Limerence, Love Bombs & Loneliness

CAELYNN MARGARET HARPER

CAELYNN HARPER ENTERTAINMENT LLC
MADISON, WI

Copyright © 2022 Caelynn Margaret Harper
All rights reserved.

ISBN-13: 979-8-9875928-1-6

Book Cover by Caelynn

Edited by Kayla-Jane Barrie, Editor and Therapeutic Poetry Facilitator

Cover Font, March, Copyright Din Studio, licensed through their E-Pub License

Published and distributed by Caelynn Harper Entertainment LLC
www.caelynnmargaretharper.com

Printed and distributed by Lulu Press, Inc.
www.lulu.com

Contents

Thanks	4
Prologue	5
Disclaimer	6
Loneliness	9
Love Bombs	39
Limerence	87
Loss	122
Languish	153
Loving Myself	219
Love	300
Last Words	363
Sources	375
About the Author	376

To my friends, Sam & Theo, who believed in me, my ability to heal and transform, and my creativity.

Prologue

This is a book of pain and processing, of healing, dying, and being reborn. Some of the topics here might not be something you want to read. This is a heavy book. But I hope it can also inspire you on your healing journey, and help you see all the ways in which you are beautiful, powerful, vulnerable, and human.

If the things you write while in pain are cringe worthy, and you still decide to publish a book on it all, that's a good thing. Some of these bits of prose I have written are raw and full of rage. Others are full of opinions and bitter anguish, based on ways I no longer think about people, places, situations. That's the thing about healing. You get all of that pus out, the blood and the fluids, and clean the wound. It is a painful process, and yet necessary, lest it fester and cause you and those around you more harm.

Still sometimes you have to keep cleaning that wound, gently, over and over until it finally closes and heals.

Express yourself deeply, fully, and speak your truth. Some might not like it. Especially if they're not looking too good in your truth, but that's not your problem. Build community, support each other, and love one another. Don't forget to also set boundaries, be open, honest, and vulnerable.

Healing cannot begin with lies.

This book brought to you by my Sun, Mercury, Venus, and Lilith in Cancer, with a Jupiter and North Node highlighting Committed Partnerships.

YOU HAVE BEEN WARNED.

Not every autistic, gay, transgender woman will have the experiences that I share in this book. Each of those groups of people are not a monolith. This is not meant as a point of data to be used to compare various kinds of women. It is instead meant as a way for me to heal, and help any who do resonate with any of this to know they're not alone, and they can heal too.

My healing has been a journey shaped by things like witchcraft and dialectical behavioral therapy, or DBT. There are many ways to heal. I want to accept my reality and who I am, while also accepting I live with other people in this world. As such, I sometimes need to change my thoughts and behaviors. This is not done to mask, but rather find a new way of both being myself, and being respectful of others. By being tactfully honest, vulnerable, and communicative, and through reflection and learning skills to cope in certain situations, I can live a life that is right for me. I can live a life that is also collaborative. I am not the only person alive, and I also am not meant to be small and convenient for others, so I must find a way of two paths, like DBT.

I am not a medical or psychological professional. I hope this book inspires you to heal, and at the same time, you need to know that I am not offering any professional, medical, or legal advice or research in this book, at all. Anything you choose to do based on this book is your choice, not mine. I also recommend that you work with a professional while on a healing journey, as this can be painful and difficult.

One more thing: this book, like healing, is not linear. I am constantly learning new concepts, being challenged and held accountable, practicing, and changing. This book will have moments where you see that raw emotion, and other times where I've learned more than I knew before. You don't need to be perfect, or get things right the first time. Aim to keep improving and holding yourself accountable.

I once gave myself swimmer's ear from crying, so that pretty much sums up the star sign Cancer for me.

1

Loneliness

Love can only find what it needs in being known, and its beauty returned. That is why it is often called a flower— without what it needs, it withers.

Solitude is a thing that no one talks about

Solitude is a thing that no one talks about
We carry the bitter pain within, silently, stilly, singularly
An ocean of dark cold water, stinging
devoid of life and light and love
Whether with others, with you, or without

Nothing changes

The ocean surges, a tsunami, tremendous and terrifying, tumultuous and turbulent
It breaks the levies, careening and coursing through the countryside
Destroying everything within its inevitable path
There once was a whisper of life in that ocean
There once was a faint ray of light
There once was a glimmer of warmth
There once
Then
Nothing

Rescue animals and me

I think the reason I want to rescue so many animals, is I see myself in them. Especially the neglected or hurt ones. Cowering when people come near, because for so long, it was pain. It was yelling. It was fear.

I still cower now.

But maybe, just maybe, I could help them heal by loving them, unconditionally, in ways I seldom was.
I'm trying to do that for myself too, every day...but some days are fucking painful.

No returns

Most of life has been without love
I love quickly, easily, effortlessly, but I am not loved in return
I think I'm damaged

To my father, who never was, thank you
Saturn returned since you left
You never did

To my mother, I love you, I know you tried
You worked hard for us, and needed to relax
But I remained hidden to you

To my step father, who was out all week for work
And drank himself angry on weekends
Life hurt you too

To every bully who threw punches and rocks
You've created a roiling wildfire within me
I hope these words curse you to be kinder

To my first love, we were poor and desperate
Not for each other but for security
We needed each other

To that same love, our hearts were ripped out
The day we lost everything
I fled, full of pain

To that old me, who drank herself stupid
You sought every comfort imaginable
You never found it though

To that first love when we found each other again
I put so much hope into a future that wasn't
For a past that ended long ago

To the countless people I have loved
I thought maybe you would bring happiness
That was unfair to you

To myself, in the mirror, sorrowful
We were neglected, and we were stuck
Things are finally releasing

Constantly struck with fear
Feeling imprisoned by a masculine body
hearing every insult on repeat in my head

"No returns", life screams at me from behind the desk
And I'm slowly realizing that that is ok

Feral

What happens when a kid who is always on their own grows up? When they're not taught emotional intelligence, and have to often fend for themselves in many ways? Are food, clothing, and shelter enough? Of course not, children need guidance on how to live on their own, how to be vulnerable and communicative, how to set and respect boundaries and autonomy and consent, and how to be emotionally intelligent.

Unfortunately, not everyone gets that kind of upbringing.

I remember in my twenties making pasta per the box. I would add barbecue sauce because I liked the taste of the sauce, and I didn't know how to fully cook food yet. I would throw together apples, peppers, and bratwurst together into a kind of outlandish stir fry, sticking to what wouldn't kill me if I undercooked it. This might not sound that bad, and I agree. It wasn't terrible, just...feral. Like a weird gremlin, I gathered up odds and ends of food that I hoped would keep me alive. I only did dishes when absolutely necessary. I didn't know how to clean properly or do taxes. I had to watch YouTube to learn basic adult skills, or use some tax software to hold my hand the entire way.

I lived. But I didn't know how to live in a way that didn't seem like the haphazard panic of someone who was a latchkey kid all grown up. I would eat Fruity Pebbles for breakfast in a Tupperware container before going to the office, because I didn't clean up much after myself and didn't know how to cook.

Before I moved out in my twenties, I had learned enough about how to socialize through trial and error during childhood. The trial, of course, was whatever shit poured out of my mouth. The error was being bullied by the bigger kids for it. I eventually learned through shame, trauma, and fear how to make others laugh so they do not think of me as "too weird". The unfortunate alternative was being just as alone at school as I was at home or in the neighborhood. That was just too much to handle.

The problem is that more often than not, I didn't say the right things from their perspective. As such, I ended up consistently alone. I didn't have much going on with people at school other than passing comments, jokes here and there, and a few friendships along the way that kept me moderately sane. I didn't have much going on at home because if it wasn't schoolwork or eating quietly at a TV tray watching Seinfeld, I was alone playing video games or constantly reading, as my main source of comfort.

Even when I was at the daycare, I was often on my own. My parents worked to pay for the blood required by capitalism, and I wasn't old enough yet to be a latchkey kid. That came later. The other kids were too young to talk to about anything, so they needed the most attention. I was there, just in case of an emergency. There weren't many conversations, other than the ones I had with myself.

I didn't know how to process all of my emotions. Quite

often, many of them were treated as "too much". Sometimes, I didn't know what I was feeling. Other times, my feelings were bigger than what was going on. Either way, I shut down. I have all of these feelings where I hate my body as it changes in puberty because I'm a transgender woman. I didn't understand it, though, the repressed Christian child that I was. I only knew there was something painfully wrong with my body, and how I was treated and perceived. Without the words to express that, I fell into depression, hoping for death, though I never tried to seek it.

That feeling of hating my body and feeling off about my sense of self never goes away.

After college, during my "feral" years, I spend any money left after bills on going out to the bars 2-4 times a week, and getting absolutely hammered drunk. Doing so makes it easier to not feel anything. The engagement that fell through, the loss of our child, the fact that I still hate the masculinity of my body and perceived self, and have no fucking idea why, all of the isolation from others I have had over the years, and not knowing what the fuck to do about these difficult emotions.

I shut myself away in my room and spent a lot of time alone whenever I wasn't at work or drinking. I didn't clean anything very often, so there was mold, decaying food, mildew towels, and smelly clothing. I was eating ridiculous food that sounds more like I used dice to choose the ingredients, or it's something that has two cooking steps–

remove and microwave.

This isn't a judgment. Low self-esteem, low energy, mental health issues, burnout from work, things pile up in all of our lives, right? In mine, though, it was clear I was having a rough time just existing.

As such, it isn't until I had a roommate who talks to me about dishes that I started to care a little more. Until, at least, we both parted ways (only as roommates, but still wonderful friends), and I was back to being a feral creature.

"What's the point?" I often wondered, too depressed to care. Yet, strangely, the shit that would lift me out of this depression eventually was caring about myself. I was still alone, but I wanted to care for myself for once after I hadn't in so long.

I realized I was transgender and carrying all of this trauma with me. I realized that it was ok to sometimes be feral when I needed rest and time away from caring so much about myself and others. But it was different now. I wasn't feral in the sense of being a child turned adult without any way to care for myself. Now, I did care. I just sometimes would have difficult days and the dishes would pile up, and that that was ok. I could get to them later when I had the energy again.

I had this different view of myself, and what I wanted from my life. I still have issues relating to people here and there, but now I know this is due to how my brain works differently than theirs. It isn't that I'm "quirky" or "weird", I'm most likely co-morbid with Autistic, ADHD, and OCD*. I'm not a "problem child" or "special". I'm someone who had different needs, boundaries, and ways of thinking and relating. I now understand myself. I now can communicate and advocate for myself.

I also know some people will not agree. They don't know my history, the things I've dealt with, the issues I have had with work and just fucking surviving. They feel entitled to call me mentally ill instead of autistic or transgender. They think it's all a phase, when they've never lived my life, nor done any research on the matter.

But none of that matters, because I know, and I'm learning.

I'm learning to take care of myself, properly clean and tidy, have healthy hygiene, and prepare food that is much healthier than what I used to make...while still sometimes making those dishes that maybe humans shouldn't eat, like barbecue pasta. I'm setting boundaries, being vulnerable, and working to communicate my needs. I listen to my emotions and honor them. When I need to, I journal or talk to a therapist about what's going on to help process everything. I am actively healing my trauma and learning to love myself.

I was never Feral. I was unprepared and left to my own devices. I was left undiagnosed with Autism, because in the 90s, almost no one was diagnosed, and the diagnoses are still heavily biased. Some days are still difficult, but at least now, I know who I am, and what I need.

I have been diagnosed by a therapist with OCD, was nearly diagnosed by my pediatrist as a child with ADHD before he was talked out of it, and Autism has been something I've determined myself, given my lived experiences. All of these, unfortunately, explain the many varied difficulties that I face with my life. There is a back and forth between the need for spontaneity and lack of focus of my ADHD and the rigid routines and difficulty switching activities and contexts and such of my Autism, with the joy of terrifying and violent intrusive thoughts from OCD, requiring constant compulsions to "feel better". It requires a lot of maintenance every day.

Messages mean trouble

I realized one day that the reason I am afraid that I'm in trouble when I get a random message from a person, is because much of the time I was ignored or left alone until I was in trouble, or something bad happened.

So now, when you get a sudden phone call, or a message from someone you haven't heard in a while, you freak out because when you're alone most of the time, and then someone contacts you out of the blue, you ask yourself, "what did I do?" Or "Who died?"

Desert

How much faith in love
Can I stubbornly hold onto?
While every passing day
Is another reminder
Of what I have not found.

Am I doomed to wander alone?
Shuffling along the dusty ground
The desert outstretched before me
An ancient ocean bed long dried up
The memories of flowing water
Without an oasis in sight.

The sun beating down upon me
The exhaustion of heat on my body
A constant reminder of danger–
Disaster is all around.
Can I survive this wasteland?
Why do I amble ever onward
Hoping for water over the next dune?

Easier now to just collapse
And let the sand and wind and heat take me

I cannot give up

Why not?

I don't know.

With a dry and heaving sigh
I take another step
And another
And another

Eternally searching for that oasis

Loneliness

There's a crushing gravity in knowing
No one owes you their time and presence
You understand this, and yet
All you know is the molasses like depths
Of bitter loneliness

It's a song composed of long rests
With interludes of brief staccatos of notes
And then back to the drawn out silence
Is it so wrong to want sound and music?

I want to see
I want to be seen
I want to hear
I want to be heard

Anything

Anything,
But the lifelong silence of a winter storm
Beautiful and dangerous
Cold and bleak

"It's your attitude
Just be around people then

Conform

You'll be less lonely then."

Shitty advice from people never abandoned
Nor felt lonely within the lies of their masks
The desperation that comes out of their mouths
Scripts used to appease others
While they fill their hearts with sorrow.

Is it my attitude?

Somedays are easy and beautiful
Others, a meaningless trudge
Attitude may do with it
But changing my attitude some days is an impossible task
When my heart hangs low
Squeezed by the anguish of longing for companionship
Someone to relate with
People to commune with
Friends and loves to share my life with

Surrounding yourself with people
Somehow, doesn't cure loneliness.
Platitudes and bullshit that fix nothing
Yet we parrot them as if they were comforting
Meaningful

Being alone is beautiful–
Why then is loneliness so crushing?

Disposable

I have spent my entire life feeling like I was disposable to everyone around me. I would be kind and caring and giving and then I was neglected, abused, abandoned. My heart is broken. I've finally reached this point where I feel a lifetime of heartache culminating and I don't know to what. I hope it's healing. Understanding. But right now, I'm exhausted. And sometimes I don't know why I'm here.

Haunting my own home

They say you die the moment
No one remembers you
I've been dead most of my life
Walking forgotten every day
Clinging to people hoping
They will surely remember me
In time, though, once again I find
Even they fall silent too

Am I so forgettable?
Or am I just toxic to them?
No one ever seems angry though
Just eternally busy
Then I slip beyond the veil
To them I died, a ghost remembered
Not a person they can reach out to
A legacy of a time before

Nothing more.

My mail is bills
Notifications selling goods
Not a message from a friend or love
Maybe once every few days
Otherwise it is just me

Haunting my own home

Damned if you do...

I get that being alone and feeling lonely is likely corrected by good, secure, community, and love. It's not so much that you want someone to be your everything, or to fully rely on others and never yourself, but without others, without love, it feels empty. Abandonment trauma is often healed by people who stick by you.

I have some of that, and yet I still have these deep traumatic pains from being ignored consistently, overlooked, being alone, abandoned, and from being left out. I know no one owes me a damn thing, it just still hurts, and sometimes, I don't know what to do with it.

I have felt limerence, I have felt hopelessness, I have held onto nothing for longer than I should, and I've learned the painful way that holding on doesn't work. And I often repeat these lessons like a fool. Every time I come back to a simple question. Who wants to be wanted by someone who either doesn't want them, or won't try if they do want them?

I want my feelings to be reciprocated, and where I understand that that's what's going on, because goodness I cannot understand half of how flirting works, or maybe even any of it (...oof do I not fully get it sometimes unless it's obvious). I overthink it or miss it or think the wrong things are flirtatious. It's something, that's for sure.

I don't want to lose hope. I see people heal and find themselves and love, I see people be in love, I know it exists, and yet I just feel...listless. Aching.

And the common denominator is me. I don't know what to do with that.

Maybe I need to let go of these ideas of love and try to be free on my own, but damn if the loneliness isn't painful sometimes. Also, I think I just need to slow down, I'm so anxious and afraid all of the time, that time feels like it's passing me by. It's not though, I mean, yes, it is, but not at some pace where I can't just enjoy each moment and take life at a leisurely pace. Just like everything else, it's difficult sometimes to even do that.

I'm learning the difficult way how to feel through all of these painful feelings, and become more resilient and patient and kind to myself. It's taken a lot of crying and journaling and spiraling to get here, and I'm sure there will be more. I think, finally, I'm becoming ok with that.

Boundaried loneliness

You can be good with being alone *and at the same time* be lonely *and at the same time* have hope for something beautiful and fantastic in the future *and at the same time* not place expectations on anyone *and at the same time* do what's best for you, and take care of yourself.

Is it confusing? Absolutely, welcome to boundaried loneliness and dialectical thought processes.

Loneliness

Walk in the woods

I walk these quiet woods alone
As I am oft to do
A somber midday stroll to calm
My weary broken heart
I come across a fallen log
And sit there for a spell
I rest my head within my hands
To cry this afternoon
The sun that now begins to set
It beckons me back home
I thank the woods for rest and solace
Before I set out on my own

Hide and seek

All I ever wanted
Was to be seen for me
With every rule and law
Further away I hid
Every time no one listened
I retreated more
Every time no one asked
Deeper I sank
Sometimes I cry out
Rarely am I heard
And never found
All too often now
I feel as though
No one is looking for me

Emotional loneliness

One of the biggest reasons I have felt so lonely is that I felt unseen. When so many of my emotions have been ignored, ridiculed, punished, or dismissed–"I'll give you something to cry about", "can't this wait, I'm busy", "fine, have it YOUR way, we're leaving if you can't stop, you EMBARRASSED ME in there!" "Stop it, it's NOT that big of a deal!!"–it becomes difficult for me to understand how I'm feeling, have the courage to be vulnerable, have healthy boundaries, respect others' emotions and boundaries, or trust people within my relationships.

When no one tells you why these things happen, why people hurt you, why people leave, and so on, you just build up these unhealthy reasons in your mind.

"I'm not enough."
"I'm too much." (Weird how you can be both)
"I'm unwelcome."
"I'm unwanted."
"I deserve this."

For so long, these are what made sense, even though they were not correct. I built beliefs around these, habits around these, routines around these. I always felt lonely, because I was. How do you feel connection if you feel unworthy? If you feel everyone doesn't care how you feel?

Often, you don't.

Masquerade

Every mask I ever don
Has always been just me
A way to hide my world inside
From those who would control me
Protection
Brought in by many faces
When you ask
Which is me
It is all of them
Each a different facet
I am always me
I don't lose time
Or memories while different
I don a different mask
You see
To protect me from those
Around me
All the ones
Who truly wish
I never was authentic

Driftwood

Driftwood, Driftwood, May I be
Drifting thoughtless on the ocean foam
I don't want to be a person anymore

Life has gone all driftless
Swaying, floating, sinking now
May the ocean roar and carry me away

Swiftly sweetly sailing home
Into Oblivion's waiting arms
May I be her lover e'er more

I don't want to live just to slowly fade
In some woe begotten slog
Fuck it all, may the ferryman be paid

If only I had the coins to lay

Maybe

Maybe you're not too much.
Maybe you're not too needy.
Maybe you're not codependent.
Maybe you're lonely because the people you fall for just don't love you in the same ways you love them.
Maybe anything other than thinking that you do not deserve love.

That's ok. As much as it hurts and it hurts so fucking bad, like a gnawing in my own chest and I just want to claw and claw and claw my talon-like hands deep into my chest to rip out the bleeding gnawing void within but you can't.

You can't.

You just have to feel it. You move through that pain, that sorrow, that bitterness, that fear, that loneliness, saying what you want until you find someone who feels the same. Maybe that doesn't exist. I don't know. Maybe I am hoping for a world where I can feel loved, appreciated, validated, understood, and welcomed.
I just hope that when the tears stop and the last one drops, that I'm still here to know the answer to the gnawing within, that I'll see what happens when you make it through that inner alchemy from one elemental being to another.

Loneliness

Can I make it?

Can I turn my own personal lead into gold or will I be consumed by the fires of purification, another lump of shapeless metal heaped on a garbage pile of history, left alone until the next time the bellows fire and I live again?

Maybe I'm overthinking things. A spaceship out of fuel drifting in the void of my own mind as the food and oxygen run low, somewhere between the hope of discovery and the panic of a loss of self. Each breath an exchange with the O2 meter on the dash and I wonder how long I have before I'm found. Maybe I will be found by a passing ship before this becomes a floating metal sarcophagus amongst the stars, drifting endlessly until the heat dissipates in the universe and it too dies.

Maybe I should sleep. I'll probably feel better tomorrow.

Cycles of pain

Just when I think
My heart cannot love again
That the pain has finally just done it in
My heart opens and I love
Only to feel a worse pain than before

And

Just when I think
My heart cannot love again
That the pain has finally just done it in
My heart opens and I love
Only to feel a worse pain than before

And

Just when I think
My heart cannot love again
That the pain has finally just done it in
My heart opens and I love
Only to feel a worse pain than before

And

2

Love Bombs

Love, by its nature, must never seek to possess, harm, or control.

Breadcrumbing

There is this fundamental difference between someone who is busy, and still makes you feel valued, and someone who doesn't value you, yet keeps you around for their ego. They use a tactic to keep you around, seeming just invested enough that you want to hold out. Maybe they'll desire me soon, maybe they'll change and take me on a date after they sort out whatever weird situation they just brought up, maybe they'll ask me out when they finally end it with their partner, maybe maybe maybe maybe maybe maybe maybe maybe.

Eventually, you conclude that it isn't working out, as you don't feel valued. You might feel humiliated. Don't–things take time for us to notice. Especially if you thought it was going somewhere, and it doesn't. That can hurt, and it's ok to feel it.

I would love to be the heroine here and say I was always kind and didn't do this myself, but I have breadcrumbed and been breadcrumbed.

Honestly, I probably deserved it.

"Why do they breadcrumb?"

I could delve into multiple reasons about it. I even thought about doing so for this–and typed out a few reasons, but I think it isn't necessary. It comes down to a lack of confidence and security most of the time, and you don't need to stick around to try to help them with that. At least, that's what it was for me. I lacked the confidence to be straightforward and honest. I've since learned my lesson, and I'm learning to be more upfront about how I feel.

If you breadcrumb, you should do the same. Have the confidence to say how you feel. Don't feel like you have to people please. Don't act like this will save someone from pain because it will not. Don't use someone to make yourself feel better.

This isn't to shame or say anyone is wicked. Sometimes it happens—we're scared, we have trauma, and it's difficult to be open. The thing is, we owe it to ourselves and others, to be honest about what we want. If you've done this without wanting to hurt anyone, stop. Recognize it, see how you hurt others how you didn't want to, learn from it, and don't shame yourself for it. Understand what you are feeling, and release it.

If you're doing this intentionally—seek therapy.

If you are being breadcrumbed, invest less, set boundaries, and if needed, walk away. You deserve to have your needs met. Also, if that's not happening here, they're not breadcrumbing you, and you still feel like your needs are not being met—you can let this go and find someone who will, right? You don't need to shame yourself for having not done this sooner. It's not always to see this right away, and sometimes it takes time to build up the confidence to do what we need for ourselves.

"How do I know if I'm being breadcrumbed?"

That's an excellent question, and it's difficult to answer. We have to be careful that we're not just always assuming malicious intent, because then you'll always find it, eventually. Instead of assuming or pulling the tarot on someone, we can just communicate with them, right?

Even so, if you're unsure, here are some questions you can ask yourself:

- *How long has it been since they spoke with me, and how often do we talk? If we talk often, it's probably not breadcrumbing. If it's on on on and then off for long periods...it might be. Especially if they're gone for weeks or months and then all of the sudden it's "heeyyy". That always seems untrustworthy to me, unless it's like friends or family or an acquaintance, you know? Even then, you can keep them at arm's length depending on how you feel about it. Trust your gut.*
- *Do they only ever seem to reach out when they need something from you? If so, it might be.*
- *Are you generally talking a lot and suddenly they're quiet? Maybe, maybe not. Remember, things come up.*
- *What is your intuition saying? Not your ego and past wounds.*
- *In general, do they feel available? Emotionally as well? It's important to note that no one can ever*

be available all of the time. People need to work and eat and sleep and have their own time with themselves and friends and hobbies and such. You are not meant to replace all of that.
- *Does it feel like there's a give-and-take or a one-sided conversation? Do they feel they are barely responding?*

These can help you get a better picture. Look not for a single example to allow you to spiral into your fears—"SEE? I TOLD YOU THEY DON'T LIKE US!" Instead, you're looking for repeating patterns of behavior. Sometimes people are busy. Sometimes we assume too much due to past trauma. Sometimes things come up. Sometimes they don't have the energy to talk. Lastly, sometimes we're the ones who are toxic and they're using the "grey rock" method on us.

It's important to look at our behaviors too. Are we triggered after we don't hear back within minutes? That feeling is valid and comes from pain. That ache requires us to sit with it, feel through it, work through it, and heal it. We cannot require someone to be always on for us. Again, no shame—trauma sucks and it takes a lot to heal it.

Sometimes, when I'm afraid that I'm being breadcrumbed or ghosted or whatever, I remind myself that people are busy. They're living their own lives. They have shit going on, and in many cases, it's not malicious. It's scheduling, it's chaos, it's burnout, it's needing time and space for themselves and others, and it's that they don't notice it themselves. Maybe if it's been a while, reach out yourself, and see what's up with them. They might be more talkative again.

If there are issues, we have ways to correct them. We can set boundaries. We can communicate our needs. We can invest less energy or walk away if we need to for ourselves. We all deserve honesty and vulnerability and communication, that goes both ways.

This isn't to shame or gaslight or minimize–sometimes we are being breadcrumbed, and sometimes we are not. Sometimes we are breadcrumbing someone, sometimes we are not. Having been on both sides, I hope this can help you discern and find ways to be more communicative and work through issues that arise.

If you're breadcrumbing someone or being breadcrumbed, maybe it's time to say the difficult thing of "hey, this isn't working out". Who wants to agonize over these things forever? Who wants to drag out something that they're not liking or are not really into?

I don't. Not anymore.

Rocks

I remember being betrayed by two kids I thought were my friends when they started throwing rocks at me on the playground, and one struck me in the face.

I learned some important lessons that day.

Not everyone you spend time with is a friend.

Not everyone you spend time with is good for you.

Frustration

It is so unbelievably frustrating that people keep needing to be taught love and empathy and authenticity over and over and over again, myself included.

The real monsters

The real monsters are not those of us who are LGBTQ. No. The real monsters are the ones who call us monsters, and then think it is ok to torture us in conversion camps, harass us, shame us, assault us, abuse us, and call us predators. All while they forced us to read about rape, incest, and child marriage in their so-called holy book.

I remember creepy stares from pastors and male teachers at the girls in my grade, from the time of about 5th or 6th grade on up. They would lean in incredibly close to them, and would not do the same to those who were boys, or at the time, looked like a boy. No, for us, we were hit, slammed against walls, thrown out into hallways, and screamed at to "toughen us up and teach us respect". Or maybe I just got that treatment.

They would stare down the front of their shirts.

I still remember that.

Sometimes it was comments about how old they looked now.

And the church always knows. They cover anything up, they try to change laws about the statute of limitations for reporting sexual predation, their politicians are changing laws to make child marriage legal, all while they scream about how we're the monsters, we're the predators.

I might not live to see 40. And I know exactly what kind of person it will be that kills me.

The worst part? I'm sure some liberal Christian will go online after I'm killed and say how unfair it is to call out Christians because "not all of us are like that". Correct...and yet you'd rather police what people talk about when it comes to the harm many fascistic Christians have done, than police the actions of those fascistic Christians.

You are no better than them, and your complacency against them, and vitriol against those of us calling them out, gives them all the license they want to do whatever they please.

Whatever happened to "Love your neighbor"? I only knew love when I did what they wanted, lived how they wanted, pretended to be what they wanted, upheld what they wanted, thought like they wanted, talked like they wanted...otherwise I was punished–and guess what? That's not love.

That's manipulation.

I am not the real monster.

What a stupid game

Admit it
You only wanted me to text so that you could play more games
That's what you do
Use me when you're bored
When you're angry
When you're alone

Even as friends, this seems like it's just a game to you
Like I'm an emotional support friend
Only useful when emotionally necessary
What kind of friendship is that?
What could this possibly even mean?
Is my friendship and trust a joke to you?

I understand that when I needed space
That that could have hurt - I hurt too
That's why I had to walk away
To let go of any expectation

Yet even as friends, you confuse me
I don't feel like you want to be friends
Or anything really
Maybe you asked me to text back out of spite

You say I miss you but do you mean it?
Are you just manipulating me?
I don't need another person doing such

Love Bombs

If I have to walk away again
I will

I have no qualms anymore
See my anger protects me
Gives me strength
I denied it for so long
Played nice with the people who hurt me
Used me
Discarded me

All when I had the power to discard them first
Maybe I am avoidant or perhaps I am bruised
But if I must use my abilities to protect myself
Then I will

I am not something to be owned or used
I am my own person
I will set any boundaries that I need
And tear them down as I will

And no one will tell me otherwise

Deny, attack, and reverse victim and oppressor

Why can't you consider my feelings?
Can't you see how you're stressing me out?
You say that you're just living your life
But you don't care how your choices impact me
You're so selfish, why do you have to do this now?
You never care about how I feel, you just carry on
What will our family think? Grandma? Grandpa?
Do you think this is fair to them?
We always do what you want to do
Why do you have to be so sensitive?
I'm just kidding, quit attacking me for it
Quit being unreasonable
You're doing all of this to get a rise out of me
You just want to see me in pain
You want me to cry
You want me to hurt
Why are you so terrible to me?

—

Stop it
This is harmful
Can't you see how you're attacking me?
Can't you see how you're making me out to be the oppressor
While you're still harming me?

Love Bombs

Even if you're confused and afraid
Your expectations of me don't match up
You opinion is baseless
I am my own person
Separate of your expectations or opinions
Even if how you feel is valid, that does not dictate reality
It does not allow you to guilt or shame me
It does not mean that you are correct
I will live as I see fit, take it or leave it
I respect your input, but I do not have to follow it
Let go of expectation
Let go of opinion
Respect my independence
Respect my boundaries

Respect me.

Say my name

Say my name
Say my fucking name
SAY MY FUCKING NAME

CAELYNN

You don't even try
You think some mistranslated and misunderstood book
Lets you treat me like shit

All because you don't like my so-called lifestyle?

You hide behind your god
Use god to justify hate
Call yourself good
Pretend Heaven is for you
When you lie
Punish
Torture
Beat
Abuse
Murder.

You are not good
Even if your god exists
He does not exist for you
You call him Love and think Love wants you when you can't love?

Love Bombs

Tell me how that makes sense!

Take the name of science
Out of your fucking mouth
You don't even know the science
You reduce it to fit your hate

Just like your book

Keep trying
Keep justifying hate
With false data
With lies
With misquotes
When you have nothing but judgment and hatred
And you can't hide it well.

Sometimes

Sometimes I feel
That you must hate me
The way you throw my failures at me

That I am ever your great villain

Is that what I am to you?

"We just need to keep you humble"

Sometimes I feel
That you still see me
As that sad, broken masquerade of a man
And not as the healing woman

That I am a joke to you

Am I just your punchline?

"You're being too sensitive"

Sometimes I feel
That I keep picking
The people who hate to see me grow

That project their insecurities

"Why do you do everything incorrectly"

Love Bombs

I know that I've done wrong
For that I am deeply sorry
My intentions and excuses mean nothing
I am learning and growing

I'm sorry that I ever hurt you

I'm not your joke, I am a person

Sometimes I fuck up and learn
That doesn't allow you to harm me
Just as I should not harm you

If that doesn't work for you

So be it

We all walk our own path

I swear there's a word for it

I expect
That everyone leaves
That I am to blame for everything
That I am unworthy of love
Of any sort of security or affection

I don't remember a lot of the affection
I remember the punishments
The yelling
Being alone.

When I was five, I rode my bike
As I often did
I was talking to people at a park
When a cop came and took me home
My mom had called them
Once home, I was spanked
For doing the same thing she glorified
Exploring the neighborhood
I learned a lesson that day
Downplay my own emotions and needs
For her own

I remember the constant screaming
The "communication"
Where chairs were broken in anger
Constant threats of leaving and divorce
Unending pleas of violence

Love Bombs

Please hit me, I dare you
Don't tempt me
I learned a lesson every time that happened between them
Stay quiet and out of sight to stay safe

There was a teacher I had
Whose family I would spend time with
Even though he threw me against a wall
Even though he threw me onto the hallway floor
Even though he yelled at me too
Somehow even with that, he seemed kinder
And I didn't want to be home alone
My parents weren't home until six
Class got out at three
I was sick of being alone even then

You know what they told every teacher
Every year when school began?
"If our child acts up—
You have my permission to hit them"
A fucked up "joke" that led to actually being hurt.
I learned a lesson every year
If I brought shame on our name
I was to be hurt
Failing at anything for me was no longer an option

When I got a job, delivering newspapers
My dad joked that I owed rent
As if parents aren't supposed to provide for their kids
If I protested, he would start yelling at me

I learned a lesson in every "joke"
I wasn't secure in my own home

And anyone who offered kindness
Hospitality
Security
It was all a lie
They only wanted something from me after all

As I was cornered, naked, in the locker room showers
After football practice in high school
I was pissed on as they laughed and called me names
The coaches never did anything about these things
I learned that security and safety were for favorites
Those with privilege and some kind of status
Never for me

My dad would joke that my food was his
And got indignant if I said no
My mom once whipped open the curtain
While I was showering
To yell at me about an airbrush
Looking like a hash pipe
The kids she looked after
When she ran a daycare
Would break my stuff
My feelings on the matter were ignored

My stuff was not mine, but everyone else's
My privacy was not mine, but everyone else's

Love Bombs

My body was not mine, but everyone else's

I learned a lesson over and over
There was no security
There were no boundaries
I was just another fixture in the house
My ideas, opinions, and feelings
Only mattered if they matched theirs
Or brought some kind of honor or good to us

So much for the Christian love I was taught
From all of these good Christian people.

Any time I brought anything up
It was forgotten or denied or dismissed.

People pleasing happens
Because you have to do it

Or else.

Lightning Rod

I am a lightning rod for others' pain
They strike at me when they are hurt
I love you
I want your pain to be heard
Please heal
Stop hurting me

Microaggressions...and maybe just aggressions

I think you'd make a good parent, that way you would have less time to think about your...fetish of pretending to be a woman

Are you a God-given man?

I saw in a documentary that the surgeries are not safe or viable. No, I didn't research that further, why would I?

When you were a man...

Are you sure that you're...whatever...you just said? I mean, maybe you're just schizophrenic or depressed.

The only reason you want to get surgeries and enhancements and such is society. "Oh, do you hold cisgender people to those standards?" What? No.

Dude! My guy! My man! Man, bro! "Really?" I say that to everyone, they're gender neutral. "You have never said that to any of our women friends." Well, no, that would be weird. *I don't mind the words if people **mean** them in a gender neutral way, and **yes** I'm **very** good at telling the difference once I know someone well and how they treat people.*

Yeah, but, are you a REAL woman? Prove it. Let me see.

Someone stares at me constantly in public.

Men are clearly better than women at anything athletic, so you being a man means you can't be in women's sports.

I think you're being too sensitive about all of this, I should be able to say what I think without you getting all offended. It's not my problem that you're hurt. *What they're saying is "me being able to do whatever I want, regardless of how it affects people, is more important than your pain".*

You should change your voice, then I wouldn't call you sir.

What is a woman? "I don't know, why don't you tell me?" They then use misogyny to define women.

Too bad you still look like a man.

What are you?

Ew, why would I date someone like you? You're not a real woman!

You're not a real woman. *Ope, guess I disappear now.*

Freak.

You're a groomer/pedophile/predator if you are gay or say you're gay around kids. *By just existing and admitting that I exist, in a world with kids?? Make that make sense.*

You're confused.

You have a mental illness and need real therapy.

You need a lobotomy.

You need conversion therapy. *This is a recognized form of torture* that uses psychological coercion and indoctrination over months and months to try to make someone straight or cisgender. Similar to brainwashing or soviet re-education camps. Run as for profit by Christians.*

You should kill yourself.

Every one of you should be killed.

I hope you're one of the ones that kill themselves.

You're a sinner and an abomination.

People like you shouldn't exist. *Never mind that we have for 5000 years of recorded history.***

—

It is so easy to just treat people to their gender. It's right there. Just treat them the exact same way you treat cisgender people of their gender. If you have questions, ask politely, don't assume. Oh, and stop talking about other people's bodies and medical procedures, as if you know better than them, or as if that's all that they are. It's disrespectful and disgusting.

*Madrigal-Borloz V., Practices of so-called "conversion therapy": Report of the Independent Expert on protection against violence and
discrimination based on sexual orientation and gender identity** (A/HRC/44/53*). UN Human Rights Council https://documents-dds-ny.un.org/doc/UNDOC/GEN/G20/108/68/PDF/G2010868.pdf

** As for Transgender history, you can go back to Sumer, in Ur, 5,000 years ago and find the priests and priestesses of Inanna who would transition by wearing clothes, taking on names, and even singing in the styles of their true gender identity. They of course were not called "transgender" as there wasn't English then, and people will try to use that to say "that's not the same", but I think we can all add 2+2. Inanna, later known as Ishtar, was even praised in an Akkadian hymn as changing men into women.

I sourced this from Wikipedia, and will include further sources from Wikipedia below.

Inanna. (2023, January 12). In Wikipedia. https://en.wikipedia.org/w/index.php?title=Inanna&oldid=1132467123

Leick, Gwendolyn (2013) [1994], Sex and Eroticism in Mesopotamian Literature, New York City, New York: Routledge, ISBN 978-1-134-92074-7
Roscoe, Will; Murray, Stephen O. (1997), Islamic Homosexualities: Culture, History, and Literature, New York City, New York: New York University Press, ISBN 978-0-8147-7467-0

But they're family

There's this gut wrenching feeling that happens when you're finally open about yourself with your family, they turn their back on you. A family raised on the words "Love your neighbor", yet avoid you more than the actual COVID plague we were going through. All because I am transgender.

One even looks at you and says "FUCK THIS" while you're standing at your adopted grandpa's funeral.

I guess adoption doesn't make you family. "Love your neighbor" doesn't cover being authentically you. If there was an anti-trans mask, they would have worn that all day, and not a single complaint about breathing would have been heard.

"Well it's all so sudden, you can't expect us to just be ok with this!"

Weird how most of my friends did. Were some surprised? Yes. Did they avoid talking to me while I sat alone during a funeral lunch, only joined by *one* of my cousins-in-law for a bit, who treated me with respect? No, thanks Kim. I felt a bit better that day, because you treated me like I was still human.

You didn't talk in hushed tones in groups, looking at me as though I were some kind of exhibit. You didn't avoid me unless I directly talked to you. When I did talk to some of them, they looked at me like I was a nuisance. You sat with me and treated me like I was still me.

I don't talk to that side of the family much anymore. If they reach out, I'll talk. Most don't. Some stalk my Instagram, but never say a word, like they're owed a view into my life without actually interacting with me.

Some acted as though I overreacted when I removed them from my socials, even though they never reached out, and ostracized me at a funeral. I just finished their work for them, and apparently, they didn't like that all too much. They're allowed to look at my life while doing nothing to be in it, like I am entertainment to them. Fuck that.

If you go through something similar, even if you're not trans, you are perfectly allowed and also encouraged to set boundaries with family. Especially if they treat you unkindly, unfairly, or without respect.

Quit being dramatic

It's not like he ever hit me
Not squarely
I still love him
I don't know why
He's nicer now
After the heart attack
But I keep my distance
I know better

He only would flick my ears
Spank me
Yell and yell and yell
Throw things
Pull me around hard
But never hit me
Maybe the back of my head
Open palmed
Never a fist though
Not hard enough for a bruise

That makes it ok…right?

I don't know
In his mind, this was nothing
He had it worse he once said

Must have been pretty bad.

Love Bombs

Everything I do is to try to make him proud and love me
I don't know why the words never seem to feel real
He could even say them but I don't feel it
How can I?

I'm not seen or listened to
Until I do something wrong
Then I wish I wasn't seen or heard at all

I know what people might say
You didn't have it that bad
Calm down
Quit being so dramatic

But if I were truly safe
Unconditionally loved
Why was I so afraid to come out
I knew the consequences that might happen
If I told them I was gay and trans.

Why so critical

I don't understand spending so much time criticizing others when they're not harming anyone. I have had so many people try to debate me quitting my job to write this book, being trans, who I love, who my friends are, and how I practice my own witchcraft. I mean this fully–fuck you, and mind your own business.

I don't understand how "my life is my own", is such a difficult concept in 2023. If you don't agree with what I do, don't do it. If it bothers you that much, bye. If you're actively trying to tear me down or keep me from living my life as I see fit, then you are a sad, pathetic, manipulative, judgmental person, and you need therapy. Is that harsh? Maybe. I don't think so.

Again, it's 2023, and people *still* can't just let people live their lives without butting in. Louder for the back, if it is not harming someone else, or removing their rights, then mind your business. No one needs your unwarranted shitty advice in their own life. If they need help, they'll ask.

And no, just because you disagree with their life, does not mean they are harming you. Just because you're offended by someone being gay or trans or a witch, is not actually harmful to you. Get over yourself, and stop acting like you are entitled to tell the world how to live.

Stay in your own lane, mind your own business, and stop telling people how to live their lives. And for fuck's sake, stop putting your beliefs into law, where it removes everyone else's rights. Enough is enough, you're not a good person.

Let people be who they are.

I will not be small for you

What I'm finding
In the snide comments of others
In the demeaning tones of their "praise"
In the way they disrespect those I love
Is a realization of how lonely company can be.

Who are you that you think you are so superior?
That your ways are best, and that I must bow to you?
Often I have looked up to your confidence
But make no mistake
I will not allow your arrogance

It astounds me that you feel you can reign over me
That I must listen to you and your ideas
Over my own wisdom.
What an ego you have there,
to think my ways require intervention
To think that only you know how to live
When there are 8 billion different ways
It is absurd, you are a farce, a folly of a person

The only person who is ridiculous is you
The only person who needs to be corrected is you
The only person who needs an ego check is you
Let me live as I will
Then I will let you live as you will

I will not be small for you

Love Bombs

I will not be quiet for you
Just so that you can feel comfortable
If you do not love me as I am
Then why are you in my life?

Lonely Security

When enough people fuck with your autonomy, boundaries, and security, you eventually feel like being alone is the only way to be safe. It is better to be lonely, private, hidden, and unreachable, than be surrounded by people who treat you poorly.

This isn't novel. I didn't figure this out. This is a typical trauma response to that kind of abuse. And yet we still don't recognize that. People act like you're insane for walking away, like you're the asshole. All because they refuse to consider for a moment how they have treated you.

You're not a terrible person for needing peace.

Nothing like endless debt and systemic abuse

It is so difficult to learn to love yourself in this current society, especially in America. From a young age, we are told what to do, and anything else is shameful. All because it is not conforming, not profitable, or not Christian. I have to ask, why the fuck should I care about that? Should I not be free to be myself, as long as I'm not hurting others?

I'm sick of having a difficult time taking care of myself because systems expect you to act and be one way. At the same time, I know I still have a lot of privileges. I just don't understand why we're still stuck in this hellscape when it is not working for the vast majority of us.

Everything is meant to drain us and our accounts. It is designed to make us into profit machines while we barely can afford any of our necessities. Endless meetings, difficult customers, pointless products, disappointing jobs, shitty managers, and for what? To survive, only to be thrown out once you are inconvenient. If you are diagnosed with something, come out as gay or trans, are not white, or are a woman, you are immediately treated as lesser and expendable. People are even plunged into debt just because their car won't start or they get sick.

Yet they tell us elsewhere is worse. Looking at the data shows me that that is ridiculous. People in Germany do not fall into lifelong impoverishment because of heart surgery. I am so exhausted because my mental health is being exacerbated by all of the systemic bullshit I have to deal with as a lesbian transgender woman.

This cannot last. This cannot be sustainable. We need mutual aid and communities, and white supremacy has not prepared white people for this. Meanwhile, so many other communities are and have been doing this for centuries out of necessity due to oppression from white supremacy.

The only way out is by helping each other instead of exploiting each other and looking at America, right now, in 2023, I don't see a lot of empathy anymore.

I let this happen to me

As someone who has manipulated and has been manipulated, you didn't allow that to happen, it just happened to you, and at the time, you didn't know how to handle it. That's not your fault. They hurt you. They are at fault. They need to stop doing that. It didn't take you too long to get out or walk away. It took you time to figure out what was happening, and how to safely get out of that situation.

You don't need to shame yourself for what happened to you, and how you handled it.

"But I did know, and I knew better–"

Maybe you knew of it, maybe you knew how, but when things like that happen to you, your brain doesn't go "ah, I know what this is and how to take care of this!" At least not right away. It instead goes into a trauma response, in order to ensure survival at that moment.

You don't need to shame yourself for what happened to you, and how you handled it.

It will be great when

I have spent so much time and effort on people who never did the same for me. People who would barely talk to me. Some would talk over me. Others would gaslight and manipulate me.

Still, others would never treat me as well as I treated them. And more would talk about how great things *could* be if we weren't dealing with problems which they manufactured. Why? I'm not sure. It was different each time, though in each there was a truth that needed to be said that they wanted to avoid. Of course, I'm not saying it was every person. Some people were great, and I fucked it up.

But I also wasted time on people who didn't really care about me, at the end of the day. You can tell if you say the words "it will be great when". Fuck that.

I deserve an "it's great now".

A denial of harm

It is harmful and toxic to pretend that you can never do any wrong. The same goes for if you cannot admit that you have harmed someone else. This can include being unable to reflect on your own failures, apologize for your actions, or consider the uncomfortable truth that we all fuck up and harm others.

It was in realizing this myself that I came to be more gentle, self-assured, reliable, trustworthy, and empathetic. I looked over the ways I had hurt others. I found that I had a lot of growing to do as a person. I had never wanted to hurt anyone, and yet I had. Instead of denying it, or letting it keep me lost in shame and hating myself, I faced it.

It was something that I reflected on often in my life. For a long time, I did deny many times before I finally owned up to it all. Sometimes I was still harmful because I didn't look at how I had been hurt, and how I needed to heal. I still make mistakes. I still need to make up for being a jerk sometimes, but in trying, I am more often kind.

I'm not entirely sure why violence happens, though I feel it is learned, often from the cruelty of others. It seems absurd to act like people are just like that, and others are not. It is absurd to act pious and judge people and pretend that "I could never do that" and "some people are evil". I don't think anyone is inherently good or evil, we're all just people who can be kind, and can be harmful. To say otherwise, to believe that some are just evil and some are not, is to pretend that healing can never happen. At that point, it becomes a justification for further harm–an eye for an eye, rather than something truly reformative.

It means that we might as well stop acting like anyone can be good, and punish everyone for every slightly harmful thing they do. I mean, they're evil, right? They cannot change? We may as well never hope that systems of oppression can end when we've seen them end before. Did that just happen because more good people were born? Ridiculous.

To me, what makes the most sense is that all things are a matter of culture and environment. ***That doesn't mean it was ok, or that anyone is allowed to keep being that way.*** I needed to stop, own up, and realize how I was being harmful and toxic in various ways. That is the way forward.

It is through realizing this, we each can avoid further violence, and heal. Some violence will always happen because, at every time, there will be unhealed people. Yet we can still work towards healing as many as possible, to avoid as much harm as possible. All it takes is a look at our own thoughts, feelings, beliefs, and actions, through an honest, anti-fragile* lens.

One more thing, everyone harms people in their lives at some point, it's just how and when. That's why I say we all need to admit and own up because too often I see people act like "I could never!" And then they turn around and are absolutely harming others. They talk over a woman of color sharing her experience of racism. They tell a transgender woman that she's not a real woman. They defend their bro who hurt someone after they just said they weren't misogynistic. They gaslight others after saying they could never be so evil as another person who was doing the same thing. Even therapists I see online will say things from a place of moral superiority, acting like they're never harmful.

Every. Single. Person. Is. At. Some. Point.

If you refuse to see that, you will keep perpetuating harm.

None of this is new–maybe that should be the tagline of my book–and yet it seems like it needs to be repeated again and again. So let's put in that work. Let's look at how we're harming others. Let's examine how our systems are harming others, tear those down, and rebuild new ones that start from a place that emphasizes connection, healing, and empathy, over individualism, profit, and toxicity.

* Anti-fragility is a concept about how well you can take criticism and challenges to your beliefs without taking them as a personal attack, when they are not meant to be one. Yes, sometimes people will use ad hominem in arguments, and you need to watch out for that, but someone saying "That is racist to say" is not an attack. It is crucial allowing us to have these difficult conversations about bigotry and violence, without causing further violence because we could not handle criticism or challenge and instead lash out.

Conflict is difficult for me

If I don't freeze by shutting down at the conflict and going non-verbal, then I am probably avoiding it altogether or trying to please the other person. Sometimes, I try to talk through it, and get upset and confused. I say whatever is on my brain, too often disastrous results. With all of that input, along with sensory input, and my emotions going all over the place, my brain has a hard time processing it all.

That doesn't mean that I am exempt from owning up to things that I do, either.

I just need to be better at asking for space to process. Maybe I can ask that things be done in a text or something similar instead so that I have time to process and understand. Hopefully, this could help me not become overwhelmed. I also need to work on not projecting my own issues onto others–easier said than done.

I often avoid conflict, because I'm terrified of people leaving. It's not healthy. What I need to learn is to be communicative in healthy ways, in ways that fit my needs. Then I can build stronger and richer relationships, rather than have some die out. It's just a matter of doing the difficult thing.

I don't know what to do with your kindness

It's weird to me. When people are kind, it feels weird. When you've had so many people be critical or mean, and you start surrounding yourself with kind people, it's just so bizarre. I end up people pleasing. "Oh I'm good, what do you want? I know it's my birthday, that's fine, but I want you to be happy."

I just don't expect it because I've had this low opinion of myself for so long. As such, I have felt I needed to go over the top for others to make sure they stay in my life, because why would they? So many others didn't unless I was useful.

I have acted out my insecurities in so many ways. I have felt terrified of loss, jealous, controlling, and like I had to please others. I'm fucking sick of that. I'm sick of feeling so low about myself that **literal fucking kindness** feels foreign to me.

I want to be there for myself and be kind to myself. I want to realize that I can trust others who respect me, and my boundaries, and are consistently kind. I don't want to trap myself in self-doubt and hatred, missing out on all of the good in my life.

I'm still angry

I forgive you
I say, high on shrooms
I forgive you
You only felt the same pain with your parents
I forgive you
Until the next day and the fungal haze lifts
I'm left with regret of saying it
I get where you may come from but I can't excuse what you did
I'm still angry

3

Limerence

Caelynn Margaret Harper

"I burn, I pine, I perish"
–Lucentio to Tranio, while knowing literally nothing about Bianca, whom he claims to love, in The Taming of the Shrew, by William Shakespeare

A word about limerence

There's some debate about whether or not limerence exists. There seems to be a miscommunication or misclassification. The professional that coined the word and some researchers have pushed for it to be its own thing. Still, others either don't think it exists, or that it is some kind of attachment disorder or codependency.

I am not a mental health professional, and any research I do is not peer-reviewed. I use the word to describe my issues of obsession and control over my relationships with others due to not processing my trauma, emotions, and fears. This word seems to mean some idea of that, and also starts with the letter 'L', and we love alliteration here. It seems more like another term for infatuation, than a mental health condition to me.

So as a reminder, this is a book about my processing and what I learned. It's not advice. It's not research. It's not meant to be a guide or textbook. It's meant to be art and real life and an expression of who I am and what I've experienced to love all parts of myself. I hope it inspires people to do the same.

It is a good idea to work with a mental health professional when healing, as I cover in this book it can be dangerous. You might learn unhealthy ideas, retraumatize yourself, or hurt yourself. This book might be obsolete compared to my new understanding, days after I publish it. Find a licensed therapist, with legal credentials you trust, and work in specialties that will help you heal, like trauma-informed care, or a disorder you have.

Listen to any red or green flags about them as you work with them. If they're shaming you, ignoring you, gaslighting you, red flags, find someone else. If they listen to you, expand how you see things without shame, and support your healing journey, commit to the practice if it feels right.

It is important to use critical thinking too while healing, especially while leaning on spirituality. Too many "leaders" mislead others to make money or push their ideals on the world. Some rebrand fascism or a Christian mindset, including harmful ideas based on racism, sexism, homophobia, transphobia, ableism, purity culture, and shame. Spirituality and religion can be beautiful in the proper context, through healthy teachings.

In any way that you heal, please be safe.

To summarize, I'm not a professional, this is not advice, and I know limerence is this contested term. Even so, I am using it to describe my issues with placing too much importance on people too soon due to abandonment and neglect, in an alliterative way. I'm still unpacking what exactly I went through, and how to have healthy relationships, and yet this word fits my needs.

Practice discernment and critical thinking in all areas of life.

The selfishness of wishing

How could I be upset
At that which brings you joy
The selfishness of wishing
That I could be what gives that happiness
While you give me mine
The jealousy from insecurities
Fear caused by feeling lesser
Unimportant
Is that true, or just a story I tell myself?
Trauma crashes through my mind
Like a colossal wave upon a beach
Thinking I'm unworthy
Somehow convincing myself
That I mean nothing to you–
I know this is not true.
Echos of past sorrows made present
My mind trying to protect me
Highlighting what is important
Instead it pulls me down into the bog
A body descending, immortalized
In a brutal moment long ago
I don't want to die amidst the muck and mire
Feeling low about myself
Allowing the riptide of my mind
Pull me out to the turbulent waves
Swim to the side and out
This feeling is temporary

These stories are just that–
This is not the past.
I am being unkind to myself
To those around me
With these ruminations
I am safe now, right?
I don't have to feel unworthy anymore
I don't have to make all that is external
Be my source of peace and security–

If only it could be so easy to feel secure
When everything around me
Feels like it could be swept out to sea

Every.
Single.
Moment.

Is this limerence?

Is this limerence, the way I feel about you
Or have I made you into a special interest?
All the ways in which I have memorized you
Because my mind cannot do otherwise
Something for my mind to wonder about
Art made human.
Bold, powerful, emotive,
creative, philosophical, beautiful.
How could you not be stuck in my thoughts
When you bring such joy, kindness, peace?
I have felt this way before
Or at least I wonder whether I have–
It has been similar and yet so completely different.
Still, any time I felt near to this
It ended, and I fear one day this will end the same
Intuition tells me that this feels safe
Yet my fear remains that this is not my intuition
Rather the hope that something might finally be safe.
Then again, is this intuition,
Or just something I hope is real?
Rejection stays in the forefront of my mind
It's just how this works–every one a great loss
Even for the smallest of friendships
The most minimal of change
Disagreements and misunderstandings
Feel like a funeral I must attend
To mourn the loss of one more person that I held dear

Sensitive to rejection, like my mother before me
I may have inherited such ways from her
So I have to wonder again
Is this limerence?
Or another way my mind works
That I have to learn to live with?
One more thing to mask to seem like everyone else
One more way to feel lonely for who I am.
Maybe I can find a way to hold space for all of this
Communicate my needs and feelings and boundaries
While respecting theirs and allowing my mind to be.

Some you I dreamt up

Can I scrape the memory of you from my heart?
Maybe it wasn't even you
Some you I dreamt up
Imagined, some ideal of you I created
Hopeful for something different
When so much of myself
Felt elated in your presence
Like someone I hadn't seen in lifetimes
Perhaps you are
Just in a different way
That would be like me
To confuse things like that
Maybe I can cleanse you out
By releasing this pain
Heaving sobs until I fall asleep
Exhausted and dehydrated
Maybe in another lifetime
I fear I have too many wounds
In this one

Let things be

I wish that I could let things be
Just as they are
Without taking friendships and situations
Turning them into "what if's"
Maybe I would break my heart far less.

If I finally let things be
Just as they are
I could be at peace
And witness the love that surrounds me
I would break down and weep far less.

Once I just let things be
Instead of attaching to dreams
Maybe then I would have joy
Instead of a deep ache
That gets worse every time.

Throughout

I have spent years waiting and hoping for people I had a crush on, liked, or loved to notice me, like me, and love me back. Maybe it wasn't love or a crush, but rather I thought I loved them. Maybe it was some limerent notion. Perhaps I've taken a hyper fixation or special interest in them, someone I've attached to, to feel safe. I'm not sure.

Again and again and again, seeking love, seeking approval, seeking attention.

Feeling like "if this person likes me, then finally things will be ok. Things will be secure. Life will no longer hurt."
Surprise, surprise, most of those people never really came to feel the way I hoped they would. For the few that did, yeah, it felt great, right up until it ended. Then it was this immense pain again, the pain of neglect and abandonment. That's what it reminded me of, the pain that followed me from childhood onward.
It wasn't fair of me to act like these people would save me when they were just trying to live their lives. That's how limerence gets you, I think, you don't realize you've put so much onto someone unfairly. Even if you do really love and care about them, you're so busy feeling these deep emotional feelings that rise up from wounds, rather than seeing what is. If it is mutual, then you move so quickly because you want to feel secure, rather than building a slow, lasting love.
Meanwhile, you're withering away. You're spending

years, even decades, on hopes, dreams, fantasies, what if's, and what could be's. All instead of what is, right now.

And then you realize this isn't it. Your heart breaks and cracks open and you're unmade. You're reformed from the deep, terrifying, pain that feels as though this is what finally stops your heart from beating. You take gasping breaths between heaving sobs as your body shakes. You feel as though you're drowning.

I understand it sounds dramatic, yet this is what happens when you grow up without stable love and emotional support. So many of our mainstream love stories tell you that love is supposed to be a whirlwind, not a stable, gentle, beautiful summer breeze. That love is out there, and it's meant to be messy until the ending. That it's cheesy one-liners, enemies to lovers, that someone secretly loves you—you just have to wait for them to realize it and tell you. Maybe it's that person you like.

This is what limerence feels like, as far as I can tell.

Rings

A life of rings on coffee tables
More than rings on fingers
A life of solitude and quiet
More than one lived in peace
Ever traveling
Never arriving

Pining

I spent so much time pining
Hoping that people would love me
As much as I do them
Maybe some did

At some point, though,
I realize I desire an idea
A ghost
A dream.

I deserve better than that.

I deserve to be loved as I am
No missed love and pining
In either direction

Just love, here and now.

The longing for security

I have felt so bad for so long for having these limerent feelings for others. Or maybe it is not limerence. Maybe it is a crush made more immense by autism, I am not sure. I feel there is a nuance there, but for now, I'm going to say that if you've ever felt guilt for these feelings, don't.

I spent so much time alone, needing security in my life, and I had never really had it. Between bullying, being scolded for emotions and autistic behaviors, and being alone most of the time, where would I have found security?

Looking to someone else like a lighthouse in a storm, as my security, was a way to help with that. I'm not saying that this is something anyone should do. Nor am I saying that it's healthy to make someone your everything in life—you need to have a bit of your own security too. I just want to make it clear that you shouldn't feel ashamed of it.

I think it's this fairly natural thing to happen—a coping mechanism from years of trauma. One time when I was feeling shame about these feelings, Hekate told me not to, that of course I would seek security after so much insecurity in my life.

Hail Hekate!

I would love to say that I have healed these feelings of shame and guilt fully, but I have not. I'm still working on it. Recently, my therapist reminded me that I'm allowed to have crushes on people. Absurd of me, right? The product of people guilting me for having emotions. I have anxiety about my emotions and how they will be perceived.

So, it's understandable and valid to feel that way. Security is what helps people with long-lasting bouts of insecurity, right? Deep down, I feel we all know and feel that need, and seek it out, and yet it is unfair to put so much of our needs onto someone else. Conversely, being anti-social and hyper-individualistic because of the various abusive and manipulative societal expectations is also unfair.

I feel I'm going to repeat this way too often—seek balance. Temperance. Finding a middle path between being an independent individual, and sharing your life with others. All without having someone be solely responsible for our needs, and our happiness. Interdependence, rather than independence or co-dependence.

That is what is healthy and makes sense to me. It feels like the lesson I am learning every now and again.

Something known by many others, perhaps, for a long time, and yet I finally realized it.

I don't want to shame myself for these feelings. I also don't want to overlook these lessons—I need to integrate them into my thoughts and behaviors.

It takes time to do this. Don't be upset if you're trying to be secure on your own and also interdependent, social, and desiring closeness with others. Even if you still have issues with needing more security because of past pain.

No one heals overnight.

All I do these lonely days

I don't want to let you go now
I feel that I was made to love
Yet it feels I have no choice
All I do these lonely days is grieve
I should have known right from the start
Any ideas I had of us
Were merely dreams

It will hurt less now than later

Many times, I have hoped for something that didn't exist. I made up these hopes and dreams in my mind, that didn't fit reality. I kept feeding into that hope, instead of being present and seeing things as they were at that moment.

After each time, I had to pay that price in pain and healing. I had to release all of that hope in tears, destroying that hope, and rebuilding a new understanding. I had to learn to accept what was real, and not daydreams. This happens to a lot of us. We "get our hopes up" as the saying goes, and when it doesn't go well, we're left looking through the wreckage, trying to find that black box wondering what went wrong.

For me, it hurt because I did this to myself, and I was angry at myself. "How wonderful it will be if they like me as I like them!" When they didn't, I had to deal with the fallout–trying to make sure that it was something I was responsible for, and not them. I had to learn to release that anger and pain I had for myself, with compassion. I still had some resentment toward myself and had to learn how to release that too.

It's not easy, especially with everything I've gone through before. Each time doesn't get much easier either. That's ok. Sometimes you have to relearn a painful lesson to understand something new. I just wish I could get the fucking point from the universe so that I don't have to learn again.

When the Tower card appears, listen. Get out of the tower before lightning strikes. Recognize when something is over, and don't stick around for hope. It will hurt less now than later.

It wasn't just limerence

It's not that every situation where I over-invested was limerence. There were times when people would breadcrumb, would play hot and cold, would love bomb and then ghost.

So now, I am looking at the ways in which I have made something out of nothing or over-inflated the importance of a situation. I am also not blaming myself for everything that has ever happened. Sometimes it was me. Other times people would invest with me and then just drop off, or keep me around in *just* such a way that it took me too long to notice.

I think I have a solution:

If it's consistently confusing, something needs to change.

Let's break that down further:

Are you consistently comparing yourself to others?

Are you consistently putting yourself down?

Are you consistently considering if there's someone else involved?

Are you consistently consulting the tarot to get

information that they're not sharing with you?

Are you consistently questioning how they feel about you?

If the answer to any of these is yes, ask a follow-up:

Are they causing these issues, and how? If so, can you communicate with them? Do they work with you on it? If not, is this something you are causing? Is it some past trauma or pain that needs to be healed?

Pretty straightforward...not always easy to remember or follow.

"What if they do like you and they're confused and not communicating how they feel?"

Yeah, that happens, I understand. The question is, do you have to wait for someone to hem and haw their way into liking you? Wouldn't you rather want someone who wants to be with you? I know I do. Finally. I used to wait and wait, because I thought that if I didn't, nothing would work out. What I was doing, though, was putting off any potential with someone who would like me and be up for being with me, for something that didn't exist.

Why don't we deserve someone taking it slow, getting to know us, being consistent, being vulnerable, being honest about how they feel, and being certain of what they want and where they want this to go?

I feel like that sounds so much better, don't you?

"Maybe you're too afraid and your guard is up too much."

If it is, I got here for a reason. I was hurt enough by people, intentionally or otherwise, to where I needed to protect my heart from situations like this. Also, if someone is genuinely interested and cares, don't you think they would take the time to show you? To invest in you? To be safe?

I would hope so. That's what I'm banking on now.

I have been unfair

One of the more difficult realizations is how possessive I can be. It's not fair to anyone I've had feelings for, everyone deserves to be respected and have autonomy. You get so terrified that someone might leave, might abandon you, that you cling to them. Instead of dealing with your fear, with your lack of comfort, you seek solace in the relationship, and if it feels uncertain, you try desperately to make it certain. I know this has been a reason for people to leave, to not want to be my friend, be my partner, and I get it.

At the same time, there are times when you notice issues in the relationship and need to address them. There are times when a partner turns secretive and their behavior changes. Some people bring that up and claim you're being ridiculous, sensitive, controlling, and possessive. Those kinds of manipulations make it difficult to know if you yourself are being manipulative, or communicative.

I wish I could give you a good model for how to know the difference. I don't always know myself. I think it comes down to whether or not what you're doing is causing harm, and what your intent is. I think it is reasonable to want a relationship to continue and to work on things. I also think that has to happen based on trust, and if you cannot bring something up with them, that's an issue. If you have to be possessive and passive-aggressive or manipulative or something along those lines to keep a relationship going, then I think that's an issue too.

Ok, maybe I *do* have a good model for it, after all.

For me, I didn't want to see people's phones, I didn't tell people how to dress or anything like that, and I didn't want to tell people what they could or could not do. Instead, I would be too quick to want a label, too quick to want to always be around them, always be in their presence, and always be afraid of them liking someone else. I remember with one of my partners years ago I called multiple times when she was out with friends because I was terrified.

I regret that. I regret letting my fear tell me that I had to be controlling to make sure someone stayed.

But that's not how it works. That relationship didn't work out either. For a time, I thought it was that she just didn't love me. Maybe some of it was, or rather it had changed into friendship over time and not romantic. I also had to look at how I've acted, how I've wanted things to be so serious so quickly because of that same fear, that I would be *way* too fake nice? Involved? Whatever you would call love bombs, I think*. Too enterprising of her time. It wasn't that I didn't mean the things I said, I did, but they were marred by a constant nagging fear. It wasn't that I wanted to use or harm anyone. I didn't realize I was clinging too tightly to someone by avoiding a possible future that didn't exist yet, but felt real due to my anxiety.

All because I was afraid. I was afraid to be alone. I was afraid I would lose her. I was afraid I would never be loved. I was afraid I was being neglected. I was afraid I was being abandoned. I was afraid I was never enough. I was afraid that I didn't deserve love.

I was afraid of everything.

I'm sorry to myself–I deserved better from myself to myself–I deserved to love myself and not be so afraid. More importantly, I'm sorry to everyone I was possessive of.

You deserved better. You deserved a secure relationship.

I'm not sure if it was love bombing, I'm not sure if that's an intentional thing or not. It was manipulative, though, born out of insecurity morphing honest care and love for someone into something toxic because of fear, doing what I could to keep someone around, rather than letting it be what it was.

Do everything for everyone all at once

"If I don't do everything to keep people happy, then people leave or they get upset."

When do I take care of myself though? Who takes care of me? Do they? Because it seems I'm always taking care of them. Why should I hold on to someone who doesn't want to hold onto me? When do my needs get met? When do I stop feeling so burnt out?

Never, unless I stop this and set boundaries.

Idolize

It was unfair of me to idolize you
I know that now
To take my trauma and feel you were more than
Who you were
Just because you treated me like a human being
How sad is that
That I had been so poorly treated that kindness
Became everything
It's not that everyone in my life was unkind
Just enough to hurt
I made this all more complicated than I needed to
I do that often
The nice thing about all of this is that I see now
I don't love myself
Not enough for it to truly matter, at least
I worship others
Rather than dealing with the pain of a heartache
I always carry
You are a most wonderful person, it's so clear to me
In many more ways
Than the kindness and friendship you offered me
But now I know
What I truly need is to love myself, more than I have
To return to me.

Love takes time

Love is not a RomCom that is done in 90 minutes. It generally takes time to build, to feel, to trust, to open up to the idea.

When you want to be loved, you think it's supposed to happen just that fast but it doesn't. You become so worried about a future that hasn't happened already by now, that you don't notice what is.

Unmasked

A momentary silence
In between both you and me

I catastrophize
That with your eyes

You've seen me honestly

That I am broken
I do not fit

For what I've spoken
Doesn't sit

And you will hate me surely

Limerence?

If everything I thought was love
Was really just
Seeking some security
That all the intense emotions
The dreams that never came true
Tempestuous desire, roaring thoughts
Rollercoasters of elation and despair
Obsessive thoughts
A cacophony of doubt and dreams
All of it was fake
Not a bit of it love
How can I learn to truly love
What does it even feel like?
What thoughts happen for them?
How do their emotions fare?
Do I love deeper because of who I am
Or what's been done to me?

I feel I could fall into the swell of it
Carried away on a bright day at the beach
You fall asleep on a floating chair for a moment
Only to wake miles away from the shore
Am I one who's meant to be with the ocean
Or safely on the sandy shore?

Will I ever understand
Or am I doomed to repeat this
Over and over and over

Demolition

So we have to demolish this world then?

Yes.

Shame, I like this one we created. It felt so peaceful. So happy.

I know. It isn't real, though. It never was.

I know.

Tears cascade as the memories I made up of you and I fade to nothing

I know nothing

Crushes

What if I just had normal crushes? Sure, I know there were crushes I had on people for *years* that I should have let go of *long* before I did. And that stems from a lot of abandonment and neglect and rejection trauma that I was not healing.

Yet, I was still vilifying myself for liking people. As if I were this weird person for having the audacity to like someone. You know, a perfectly normal human thing to do.

Of course, I was awkward and was navigating the world as an Autistic teenager at a time when most didn't understand what that meant. A lot of people treated me as somewhat of a pariah, though I was also in most groups.

Life's been weird. To be generally accepted by all, but still often isolated because you're not fully a pariah or a popular person, is just a bizarre thing.

So I'm this socially awkward Autistic kid who is learning how to socialize better, a bit of a heavier person, and also I'm closeted transgender and queer. I had a lot going on beneath the surface, that no one could see but it seemed everyone could pick up on—to an extent. At a Christian school, in the early 2000s, that were a lot of strikes against me.

At the same time, I'm not going to say that I wasn't weird sometimes, I was. I won't say that everyone made me out to be undesirable, there were some great women who asked me to school dances and it was a lovely time. I had some close friendships, though some of those too could have an element of bullying to them. That's something that would continue for a long time.

Of course, none of them knew I was transgender, shit I still didn't know. Remember, Christian upbringing means repression, right?

Over the years, I still have these moments where people say "oh, someone like that would *never* be into you," and then would laugh or make fun of me. It's like I'm still in high school but in my 20s, into my 30s, and I'm still shaping my self-opinion.

No wonder I feel ashamed when I have a crush on someone, like I'm this lowly person. It was driven into me time and again by emotionally abusive responses to me having a crush.

Again, I have held onto people for too long. I have made my crushes out to be more important in my life than they were. I have been awkward, and weird, and have completely missed probably millions of social cues by now. I also kept terrible friends around who made me feel like I was subhuman to them.

I'm still a human, a beautiful human, a wonderful human, who is allowed to be attractive and show attraction, as long as I'm being respectful and honest. I won't be everyone's cup of tea, and that's ok. I also don't deserve to have someone judge me for liking someone, whether it would work out or not.

I'm not going to feel bad for liking people anymore. If someone tries to make me feel undesirable, I am no longer going to take that on. That's not my issue. It's theirs. I will let them know that's not ok, and if they continue, I don't need that person and their judgmental and unkind energy within my life.

4

Loss

"The only constant in life is change."
–Heraclitus

"All conditioned things are impermanent."
–Buddha

No one mourns for me

No one mourns for me
No one stops me when I leave
There are no protests, no bitter moments
Just a realization that I will be gone, and maybe an emoji or an "ok"
An afterthought–Distant and cold.

It was as though I never existed to begin with to them
Something to be used and abandoned
and should I leave on my own?
Well, that just made it simpler then

There are no follow-ups
No sad goodbyes
No begging to reconsider
And though I feel ridiculous
to want an absurd performance
At least it would mean they cared even once–

They did not.

Maybe what I felt was purely my own

Have I ever truly connected to anyone?

It doesn't always work because you want it to

Loving someone else isn't enough to have them love you too. It hurts, and that's ok.

For a long time, I thought that if I was amazing, kind, funny, and loving enough, people would love me back. Friends, family, partners...but that's not how it works. I also wasn't always as present, and I couldn't be. My Autism means that I need to sometimes be on my own, away from others, needing quiet and solitude. I know this sounds like a contradiction because I also have felt pain due to isolation, but I need some solitude, not constant solitude. I also had a hard time externalizing the millions of things I felt and thought and knew internally.

To me, much of the time, other people's needs were more important than mine. I was ignored or rebuked if I finally started to set boundaries or express needs. I was no longer convenient.

I found that I could love others deeply, and be there for them. It didn't mean they would love me the same or stay. I didn't see how this was eroding my own needs, my own sanity, my own boundaries. Things would fall apart or feel empty. Often, I'd be left wondering why.

Even if things were out of balance, I've finally allowed myself to grieve when something doesn't work out. Even if it was short lived, even if other people question why, it doesn't matter. I need to process and release all of my emotions in the way that is healthiest for me.

I'm still learning what that means for me, what's healthiest for me, and that too is ok.

I've had times when I had to release so much pain by crying after just a date with nothing further. Was it about them? No. For me, it was past trauma coming back up. That's ok too.

I have to keep reminding myself that being human is ok.

Don't let people tell you how to process your emotions, cry that shit out. Go to a rage room. Talk to a therapist. Journal.

You're allowed to feel things, even when what you feel "seems too much". You're allowed to feel things, regardless of whatever people might say to you about it. They'll tell you to get over it, toughen up, quit crying, blah blah blah. These are the words of someone who needs to cry too but refuses to let themselves release and heal. They see you healing, and hate it. To them, no one lets them do the same—and by no one, I mean they won't let themselves do it, while they say "no one lets you do that".

I will no longer let others tell me how to grieve, and I will grieve every single thing that doesn't work out.

Walk away

How do I walk away?
I've left and I'm still there
In my heart and soul
Not once, have I forgotten.

A video with your voice and I'm elated and back there

How do you do this to me?

What is it that keeps me here with you in my heart, when you're worlds away and claim   nothing of me?

Do I have to kill my own heart in order to leave?

Breathe in
Breathe out

My breath, an endless wave,
Crashing rhythmically through the pain of a hopeless love

Inconvenient

Love me
Until I'm no longer convenient
Then cast me aside.

Invite me out
When I'm no longer online
Then forget to text.

Can I trust anyone?

For so long, I have been left out
A pariah to family and so called friends
Because I am different than them

I tried so hard to be
What everyone wanted of me
Even then, I was an outcast

Maybe this is some divine lesson
To let go of everyone and everything
Find meaning in solitude

But I want companionship

Why is it so difficult
To be close to others
To find people who love me for me?

Loss

Every time I try, it ends.

It's maddening.

Does anyone else have to try so hard?
Just to be accepted as they are?

I'm exhausted.

Trying to let go of past neglect
Yet every time I turn around,
There it is.

Spent

I've spent my whole life so far
Hoping for love
Longing for love
Dreaming of love

Only to be left by love
Abandoned by love
Removed from love
Traumatized by love

Sometimes

It's difficult to remember

Why I even wanted love.

Abandonment

Just because someone leaves, doesn't mean you're at fault. If you're racking your brain, and you can't find a "Yup, I really fucked up" moment, then maybe it's on them, or might be an issue with timing or circumstances. Maybe they don't like you personally, and that hurts, but that doesn't mean everyone will be the same. And if there is a moment where you fucked up, learn from it, and be better moving forward.

You are not unlovable. You are not left behind because you are some freak or terrible person. You're kind, smart, funny, and can brighten a whole room. People love you, and you need to love yourself. Just because they leave, does not mean you are not loved.

You are. And you are worthy of love.

Remember that.

Languish

Are you ok?

Yeah—I suppose I am. This isn't the first thing that fell through, nor will it be the last.

Oh?

Is that surprising? Do some people have what they hope for?

I guess I'm just more surprised at your tone...

Oh, I see. After decades of broken promises, events called off, plans falling through, things ending before they begin, you just sort of...get used to it. You persist. Somewhere between hope and despair. Languishing.

Maybe something will work out? Surely some things have.

Some things. The small things, the little wishes. The things that help you get through the pain, the numbness. One nice thing in all of the quiet, you learn to know yourself.

That sounds nice.

It is.

Loss

So then are you that upset?

No, it's more...unsure of what's to come. I have hope now, but one day, the embers will cool as it just fades, and my heart just–isn't in it anymore. What will become of me then?

That noticeable lack of confidence

It's bizarre how people call me confident or brave. I have terrible anxiety, all the time. Panic attacks, crying, yelling, melting and shutting down, all while I try to find ways to calm down. I am afraid that my fear, my awkwardness, trauma, emotions, Autism, ADHD, anxiety, any and all of it, has pushed people away that I care about.

Sometimes, I think it has. It's absurd to feel so afraid. I know it. Or at least I know it right now, when I'm not panicking. I lost so many people along the way either due to life, time, growing apart, or their toxicity or mine. Each and every time, though, I blamed myself.

If only I was "normal" and not trans, not gay, not awkward, not autistic, not a witch, not my traumatized and broken self. People left, so it had to be because I'm weird, right? Of course not, I'm just my own person. If people cannot like that, that's their deal, not mine. I found joy in myself. Did I remind myself of that whenever I would blame myself? No. I would compare myself to others and think it had to be me. If other people could figure all this shit out, then, it had to be something about me.

In most cases, it's just what happens. People grow apart. Sometimes it was them. Sometimes it was me, though not because of who I am. It was that I didn't love myself. Didn't believe in me. Didn't trust others. Disrespected them. Years of pain just broke me down into thinking I was this disgusting thing. Even now, when I'm overthinking, when I'm panicking, when I'm overwhelmed, those thoughts creep back in.

You're not good enough.

You're disgusting.

You're weird.

You're not lovable.

Things that terrify me that they might be true. I am healing and yet it's still there.

I'm sorry to those who had to experience any part of that. Not because I am autistic or trans, or anything like that, no. I will not apologize for who I am, though some might want me to. I am sorry that I didn't believe I could be loved, platonically, romantically, or otherwise.

I held onto the belief that you couldn't love me because I couldn't. I am sorry to myself for not loving myself, and not believing in myself. I am healing because I'm finally loving myself. I deserve to be happy and confident; loved by friends, family and partners, and to be confident.

To those of you who love me, thank you. I love you so much. You have been helping me see that I deserve to be loved for who I am.

The tower trembles

Why is it so simple
For others to feel secure
When I never do
I cling to fantasies and hopes
Because reality is often cruel

Their tone has changed
It once was sweet
A pittance now, what was before

And I feel the tower tremble as the horizon darkens

"The walls are sturdy
The bricks are thick
Nothing will fell this place"

You can say it a hundred times
But I know, everything is changing
I can feel it in my constricting heart

"My love, intoxicating
Oh so beautiful
I am so drawn to you"

I was drawn too
I must admit
You were different from the rest

But here I am
Always investing more
While you pull away

You will ghost me like the rest

Wandering storm approaches
Lightning strobes
Thunder roars unending

This tower will not last.

A land full of broken castles
Anxiety, their mortar–
Trauma the very stones
Each weakened from the start
Before every one collapsed.

Forgetting a dream

How can I forget such a beautiful dream
Can such a thing be done or taught?
To forget the possibilities of light and laughter
Where before there was silence and darkness
To forget the way you lit up whenever we spoke
As if what I said was wonderful and intriguing
To forget how time disappeared, just you and I
While the universe unfolds, no matter what we did
To forget how easy it was to dance our tongues
Creating these sweet words and phrases
With or without purpose,
formulating sounds never uttered before,
Building a language no one else could comprehend?

But we awoke.
I was left with the memory of a world,
One that no longer was
Our dreams had twisted into nightmares
We could no longer walk this garden path we planted
Your voice grew silent and time surged forward
Until the silence and darkness returned

Everything we had been was no more,
As everything must become.

Rejection escapism

"Rejection is protection"

"They rejected/ghosted because your guides/ancestors are protecting you from them"

"They're only rejecting you temporarily. They're your soulmate for sure, and they're just deep in their feelings. They'll come around."

These are all *possibly* true *sometimes*.

More often than not, though, they are not. It is dangerous to keep touting these as the main reasons for rejection in spiritual spaces. Sometimes people just don't like us, and that's difficult and uncomfortable, but is true.

We don't need to sugarcoat it to make ourselves comfortable. We don't need to deny that it happened. Instead, accept that they said no, that they ghosted you, or however they have rejected you.

Accept it. Then, feel through it, and this is important, away from them. Just because they said no, doesn't mean they have to guide you through your processing of it. Understand that generally, it's not saying something terrible about you. If they gave you a specific reason that you need to work on, then do so. Even so, you're not broken, disgusting, unlovable, or whatever—even if you need to work on your behaviors and beliefs based on their feedback. We experience rejection from each other for a myriad of reasons.

Do not try to build a narrative like "well clearly, they just suck" or "I'm the worst".

Sit with how uncomfortable it is. Honor your emotions. What do you feel in your body? Stinging tears? A deep pit in your chest? Good. Feel through that. Note it. Do not explain it. Feel the emotions fully and let them pass. Once past, then if there's more information like "You kept crossing my boundaries" or "I don't find you attractive", then process that. With that first one, work on boundaries, respect, and autonomy. With that second one? That's their own preference, you don't have to hate yourself. Plenty of people will find you adorable.

When we create stories such as "Your guide was protecting you from them" we don't actually process the pain. Instead, we paint over it with a story like "actually, *they* suck", which isn't helpful. It builds that ego-centric narrative in your mind, rather than helping you grow and see reality as it is.

The toxic narratives of "I'm always right, and it's everyone else that is the problem", "They're my twin flame and they'll *totally come around*", or "I suck, and clearly no one cares" are problematic. They will continue to traumatize you and harm you. These are also generally not your guides. They are not spiritual, but instead a form of bypassing. They are not ways to draw in what you want in life through spell craft or attraction or whatever you work with.

Having done and thought all that myself, I am an unfortunate authority on the matter. I'm still processing and unpacking everything. I'm sure I will be for a while as healing takes time.

I know these things can hurt. It may feel like it's better

to escape the more painful feelings and situations, but I can tell you, it comes up eventually. The question is, do you take care of yourself with love now, or later, after you've grown more attached to the fantasy of it all?

The embarrassment

The embarrassment and shame felt when you develop a crush, and they don't want the same thing. After what I've been through, how could I have ever thought it would be this way? I know that sounds unfair to feel about myself, but it's what you need to feel through when you've been hurt again and again.

Feeling like you're worthy takes time to regain within. It's not their fault either, not everyone is for everyone. That's a good thing–it would be chaos if we all were for each other.

That feeling of being unworthy and embarrassed? You need to honor and learn from it. Then let it pass. It's a painful feeling, but it needs to be released. Sometimes I'm still learning how to feel it without becoming overwhelmed by sadness and shame. It takes time, and that's ok too.

Checkpoint

There's this checkpoint in my mind, that I keep coming back to, and I can't seem to cross.

It's a checkpoint where I realize someone isn't talking to me as much as I talk to them. I would like more effort from them, yet I know that no one owes me anything. We're all autonomous beings that have shit going on, right? At the same time, I hear people talk about how they talk to friends, family, and partners all the time. I just don't understand how that happens. What I understand in my own life, is that there are a lot of conversations with someone up front, and then they just eventually slow.

I am concerned that if I stopped talking in all of my relationships only like two or three people would sometimes reach out. Everyone else would fade out. I do not want constant conversations with everyone all the time, I mean, damn, I need time away too. I just don't understand what a normal cadence or effort is and what I'm supposed to do.

I don't know, maybe I should let the relationships that are not working fall through. Maybe I should use boundaries to only let in people who actually fucking try, but goddamn it if that doesn't sound lonely. Then again, having people treat you like an acquaintance when you thought you were pretty good friends? That can be even more painful.

No one owes me anything, but I would like it if someone would want to reach out more. I would like to have people in my life that want a deeper connection with me. That's not in the sense of platonic turning into romance. I feel we all treat romantic relationships as the only deep relationships. It's not about changing the type of relationship, but changing the investment, and the depth of the connection.

At the same time, some friendships are still deep, even when you aren't talking all of the time. I think it's not so much about how often we talk. I think it is more about how much someone invests in the relationship. It's about the energy of it, right?

Some of my friendships have that feeling of depth to them, and I'm grateful for that. I think maybe the checkpoint is passed when I stop giving time and effort to people who don't care. Even if it means I have fewer people in my life, at least the ones I have are meaningful.

Maybe I fill that time where I'm alone 98% of my life with more creativity, passion, and personal connection. At least then I'm being there for myself, and the people I have that deep connection with. I would rather that, than invest so much time and energy into people who do not care.

I think I just passed the checkpoint, now I have to remember this any time I ruminate on it.

Please let me be made anew

I am just trying
To live through this pain
Breathing deep sighs as my heart is crushed like tomatoes within
Let the juices fall as they may
A red cascade into the pot
To be turned into something new
Will I be the same?
Am I transformed through this
Or am I doomed to this?
Stir my pain and sorrows into joy and peace
Let the aching reduce into a sauce full of spice and wisdom
Rich with complex flavors and the understanding of how love works

Please let me be made anew.

Do you believe in me now?

I'll never understand it
How you could be so underhanded
It's almost as though
You never really liked me
It's almost as though
You never really believed in me

Loss is painful enough

For a long time, it was easier being mad at everyone that love never worked out with. It gave me something to point to when I felt like shit and think, "that's what's wrong."

But it was disingenuous. It wasn't really wrong, just unfortunate. Some people actively hurt me, yes. I also know I actively hurt others by not committing, ghosting, or any of the usual shitty suspects, you know? But often, more often than not, it wasn't bad like that. It just ended. Fizzled out. Incompatible.

Now, I can recognize that and still mourn. It's not like it has to be a significant loss. Sometimes these things hurt harder than you expected because it just reopened an old wound, and that's ok.

But there's no need to find some moral high ground. Sometimes things just end, and that's all it was. Neither person was the bad guy. All too often you see people call someone a "narcissist" because "he didn't want me". That's not what that means! Sure, other times, someone was a shithead and being mad as a release is necessary, though it's not in every case.

We seek to make ourselves feel better at their expense way too quickly.

I think what's important is feeling through and releasing everything. It's important to learn what you can. Maybe you need new boundaries. Maybe you find values and needs you didn't have before that you'll express the next time. If they did suck, maybe you learn a new red flag.

If you need to be angry, be angry. I am not saying you need to never feel what you feel. The question is whether or not the judgment itself is needed. Maybe it is, I'm still learning. I'm still unpacking trauma and things I learned at a Christian school, so my view is going to be unique. It will also most likely change. I am not the same as I was five, ten, or twenty years ago.

Right now, I'm about feeling and releasing emotions healthily, not in a toxic positivity sense. Nor am I about being some paladin, routing out evil with a holy cudgel, making everyone else into demons, sinners, and whatnot.

It's never that cut and dry. There's a lot of nuance to every situation. Yes, some people do shitty things, and you can call that shit out. Just don't let the people who sucked turn you into someone who thinks everyone sucks, or that everyone who rejects you sucks.

You deserve better than to push good people away because you're expecting them to be like the shitty ones. This is something I am always having to recall, because in the moment, it is easy to forget. It's not all my fault. It's not all their fault. It's different and nuanced every single time.

All of my poems are incredibly dramatic and raw. Each one, is full of emotions from the pain of loss and self-doubt and anger and insecurity. Even so, I try not to hate or judge anyone from my past anymore. I may still need to release difficult emotions, but I want to do so without acting like everyone is evil and out to get me. Something that has been difficult for me, is when I have had a lot of people treat me poorly.

We were all figuring shit out. As I've healed, I've noticed that sometimes the way I thought something went wasn't how it actually went. Perspectives change, values morph, and you see things in new ways. I might never get back together with anyone, but that doesn't mean I hate them.

And other times, I'm mad again, and processing the pain in new ways.

In most cases, I know now that maybe they weren't out to hurt me or ruin everything. They were often scared, hurt, insecure, or weren't feeling it. Just as I was. I can know that and understand them a little better. I can let them and that pain go.

This is not to say that you have to forgive and forget. This is where I, personally, am at, in situations where I was overall safe. Take my approach with a grain of salt. Use your own discernment to determine if that's how you want to approach your own past situations.

Sometimes you shouldn't forgive. You're 100% in the right for being full of rage and sorrow and needing ways to release that. You sometimes need to run and cut them out and be safe from the people who hurt you. Other times, you can work on the relationship and build it up stronger by being vulnerable with your emotions and the pain caused, and how to move forward.

Honor your emotions, and intuition. Seek wisdom from within yourself and those you know you can trust. Work through your situation in a way that is correct and safe for you.

The ghastly investigation

Did you ever really love me?
In the still nights
Laughter over meals
Our tears of loss
Did you?

And if you did

When did it die?
And why?

Or did it just change?

What do I do with these memories?
Of your laugh, your smile, the way you say everything
Are you mad that I walked away finally
Needing space to heal
I have, and yet some part of me remains back there
A ghost of us, haunting me
Something I know will not live
But remains nonetheless

Do you see the ghost of us too?

Moonlit immolation

I am grateful for every mile walked
Each and every goodbye
Another road post signaling the way
From where I was lost
To where I will thrive

I do not mourn the places and people I left
I mourn what could have been
Not what was
Each tear a release
Helping me purge all pain and anger and frustration
Until all that is left is peace

Through darkened woods, twisted branches reaching
Swamps whose lilies danced in the moon's glow
Across vast prairies, where I saw my enemies
Miles away
I made my escape

Every step
A punctuation
Ending a sentence
that imprisoned me

You see phoenixes do not die
Because they are old
But because they can no longer soar
And with their isolation

All the old ends
So they may rise anew

I wander, here and there,
Wondering about the phoenix
Its lessons on death and rebirth
Swimming through the pools of imagination
Like the tadpoles in the swamp
Making their merriment as they grow
Each thought maturing
Until I understand the lesson fully
And it leaps onward

So while I cried and bore my pain to the moon
I did not mourn, but instead was renewed
And as the moon set
Reminding me of all I lost
Immolation
Just as the sun rose

I too shall rise

5
Languish

Sometimes you need to wander and wonder, become lost in your own life and mind, making mistakes along the way. Sometimes you need to fuck around and find out.

Escape

I cannot face it
I will not
Why do I have to anyways?

I hate it here
I'd rather be there,
Much better than my own life.

You know what would be great after this workday?

Anything to escape right now.

–please I don't want to feel anything–

Why is life so painful?
Look at how they have it–
Why can't I be happy like them?

Just medicate me.

Anything but existing in this moment
Even if I have to face it someday
Please, just let me avoid it for now

Please

Caelynn Margaret Harper

I am terrified

What is yours will never miss you

Sometimes "What is yours will never miss you" is helpful. I say it to myself, and I feel assured. My anxiety calms down a little bit, and I don't feel like I'm always going to be alone, always neglected, always abandoned.

I know too many people on the outside, this may sound ridiculous that I could fear this. "I'm always a phone call away! Don't I tell you how much I love you? I give you all of these gifts!!" Yes...and also no. I don't know how to put it. I can recognize the care and the effort, I can. Yet sometimes those things feel as though there's something further attached. Something I have to do or perform to pay it back. Or, perhaps, it's only a matter of time before it sours.

I know that's not how it most likely is, it's just so much of my life has been full of transactional relationships. Relationships based on unfair expectations, conditions on love based on who I can and cannot be, manipulation, betrayal and even my own toxic behaviors. You eventually have a hard time imagining or feeling that it could work out.

When you didn't live up to those expectations? You were left behind, ostracized, punished, and held at arms' length, even by your best friends and your family. Other times? You pushed people away. You ran and hid. You were an asshole and they rightfully kept you at a distance. Some walked away entirely.

This is why, sometimes, this saying is harmful.

It's difficult to believe in such a saying when your

trauma is centered around people constantly leaving you or breaking your trust. It's difficult to believe when you see the ways in which you've hurt others and yourself. "What is yours will never miss you" sounds helpful, but at best, it is often a platitude. All too often, when people have "missed you", they have mistreated you, or you have mistreated them.

It's difficult to trust and to hold onto hope. Even when you feel that that is the only way to find peace in yourself, and in your relationships with others.

They say that the way to heal abandonment and neglect is to have someone actually stick around. I feel more and more of the people I keep in my life are here to say. I'm just still lonely and healing pain centered on the love of all kinds. I don't bring these things up, though, because it feels manipulative, even if it's my trauma. Even if it's true.

I want to feel that security in more than just myself.

Even now, almost 35 years in, writing a book about all of this, I don't really know how.

That which slithers and seeps

There are moments in the quietude
Where a creature dark and fluid
slithers and seeps from the void of my mind

It moans and cackles, it sinks its claws into my memories
and wraps it tentacles around my brain
Suddenly there is me, and the Fear Come To Life

It twists my memories like a worm-tongued advisor
Hissing and screeching its vile testaments within
Compromising all sense of who I was before

There I sit, so grey and dreadful, dead to all who knew me
Knowing what is true and yet trapped in lies
Loops of fear and rites, a waltz designed by the Fear Come To Life

It curses my eyes with visions profane
Of me tormenting the villages, a monster set free
That I was never good, but ever unholy

My evil is ravenous, my terror knows no bounds
I am and ever was the great and true destroyer
I've lost who I was to the Fear Come To Life

Am I still human, and was I ever me?
Am I capable of such terrible things?
Am I to die to bizarre circumstances?

Caelynn Margaret Harper

This is what it is and what it wants
To make you beholden to its fear
To convince you that you will never be free
Of the Fear Come To Life

Needs to be said

Not everything that needs to be said, needs to be said by me. I don't have to fix the world's problems. I don't have to center myself and save the world. Shit, I would like to be saved. I'm sick of the way that people treat transgender people and autistic people, but here we are. Everyone has said what has needed to be said about these things, yet people are still assholes.

I don't even know what I need to do anymore.

When we're quiet, the abuse happens. When we say something about it, the abuse is denied and still happens. When we fight back, the abuse escalates. It mounts to the point where people think their hatred and lies are not only correct and okay, but "under attack". They were the oppressors for getting upset at their abuse. DARVO in action, I suppose. They escalate, pass laws, shoot us, assault us, and lie about us more. They've sent in bomb threats to schools and public buildings just to keep people, who were bullying a transgender child, from being held accountable for their actions.

It worked.

At this point, what do I do? I have said so much about all of this, and have been ignored or had people argue with me. Do I move? What about all of the people who can't? If I escape, it only helps me, it doesn't solve the issue. But again, I am not the world's savior. I'm an autistic transgender woman, who doesn't need to be at the center of any movement because anything I come up with is framed from a white point of view.

I don't want a gun to protect myself, what if I kill someone I love because I think they're some kind of intruder? I have pepper spray, but is that enough? Will that stop someone who wants to harm me for just existing as I am? Will locks be enough? Should I get cameras to help people find out who hurt me? Would the police even care about me? Probably not. They don't tend to treat transgender women well.

Maybe I need more community. I'm surrounded by people who, while they love me, don't experience what I do, and don't know how to help. I try to teach them, but even I only know so much. I need people like me that I can support and be supported by.

I'm exhausted–the unofficial title of my life and this book.

I just want people to stop hating others without reason. To stop hating what they don't know. To want to control others. They don't even care, really. They've just fallen to propaganda created by those with the most, in order to keep them from asking "why are my hospital bills so high", and if they do, the response is "oh it's trans people. It's anyone who isn't white. It's not us, it's not our price gouging, blame them!"

And so, when I walk to my car at night, clutching my

pepper spray, hoping I will not die to someone who blames the wrong person for the problems in their life, at least... nothing. Nothing. I have no happy ending for this whole musing. I'm sick of being called a predator as a transgender person when I am the one constantly hunted by fake feminists, conservatives, Christians who don't even understand 0.5% of their bible, and fascists. I'm more likely to be assaulted, sexually and physically.* I'm more likely to be discriminated against. Some conservatives tell me that I should kill myself, disappear, just be normal, and then they slide into my DMs, propositioning me. When I say no, it's back to telling me to kill myself and insults.

"Feminists" post people's pictures without their permission, saying we're too masculine and pushing for patriarchal norms while using patriarchal standards of beauty to judge us. While saying that "real women" give birth—a patriarchal gender expectation. They're not "feminists" by any measure. How could they be, when they side with fascists, conservatives, and incels in order to hate transgender women?

I don't know what to do. I don't know what to say.

Maybe not everything that needs to be said, needs to be said by me. I don't have the full picture. All I can say are the small bits of information that I know, like here, and hope that it builds a full picture with others' words and we can finally move forward from all of this.

---

* *Transgender people experienced 86.2 victimizations per 1000 persons compared with cisgender people's 21.7 per 1000 persons (odds ratio [OR] = 4.24; 90% confidence interval [CI] = 1.49, 7.00).*

Households that had a transgender person had higher rates of property victimization (214.1 per 1000 households) than households with only cisgender people (108 per 1000 households; OR = 2.25; 90% CI = 1.19, 3.31). Transgender victims whose sex assigned at birth was male were more likely to perceive their victimization as a hate crime than cisgender victims whose sex assigned at birth was male. There were no disparities in reporting victimizations to authorities: only about half of the victimizations of both transgender and cisgender people were reported.

Andrew R. Flores, Ilan H. Meyer, Lynn Langton, Jody L. Herman, "Gender Identity Disparities in Criminal Victimization: National Crime Victimization Survey, 2017-2018", American Journal of Public Health 111, no. 4 (April 1, 2021): pp. 726-729.

Insecurities

I'm still trying to figure out how to want love, while loving myself, without making some expectation out of it. It's like I get so eager and so hopeful for this idea in my head that I get hurt when it doesn't work that way. Not an expectation of someone else–but rather I made something more significant in my mind, and when it isn't like that, I have to deal with the pain. I don't make it anyone else's problem.

I'm still working so hard to just have security in myself. To love myself. To allow myself to desire and be desired by someone who actually wants something. To not go for crumbs or cruelty or carelessness or the like. I don't want to feel like I'm eagerly awaiting a maybe, that the other shoe will drop, or that I have to walk on eggshells to keep them from exploding at me.

So many times I stayed when I shouldn't. So many times I didn't try. So many times, I waited for something that wasn't there. So many times I didn't believe someone could like or love me back, or that people didn't think of me like that, so the idea that this person might seem like bullshit.

I deserve to believe in myself, and that others could see me as I am, and love me. I deserve to love myself, and know that I'm worthy of love.

When spring finally comes

In the cold dark apartment
On the second floor
I await the sunshine
Of a new spring day
Where the flowers bloom
And birds return to sing
I am no longer alone.
I have warmth and bees
Flowers and rain and stars
Mostly hope, in this place, here, now
I feel...like something could be *more*

When the snow of my heart thaws
And the last bit of that water runs
To the heightened rivers
Off towards a vast ocean
Teaming with life
Maybe I can be there too
With the water and whales
Flowing and swimming and alive

Thriving

When spring finally comes

Grasping

There are old parts of me
That grasp for my body
Clinging and clasping
A horde of human hands
Holding harshly
hoping to heel me in place
Pulling me backwards
Into the depths of old pain—
Trauma I am trying to heal.

Every step forth, they lash out
Screaming and gasping
Telling me I cannot leave
It is safe here
It is better to suffocate with us
Than to try out there and die
In some unforeseen event
Gods above and below
Hear me

I just want to move.

Caelynn Margaret Harper

I don't know why I hold on to life sometimes.

Without sin

I spent so much of my life trying to appease the Christian God, hoping to be holy and perfect, but you can never be. Mistakes will always happen. Further, that entire book has laws that contradict each other and make it nearly impossible for you to be perfect. Even without some holy book, mistakes will always happen. People do not know everything they need to know and slip up all the time. Thus enters the need for a savior, and the idea of hell to motivate people into paying the pulpit to get into heaven.

My brain, other than being autistic, has all this trauma, especially religious trauma. Through that comes this drive, this need for being perfect, for not offending higher powers, and for living correctly. I have spent decades carrying the weight of my sins. These sins are not so much the markings on some dusty stone tablets, and instead more the understanding that I have harmed others.

Sin to me now is not something biblical, but a word that I can use to remind myself that my actions carry a weight to them. It is not some mystical force that tallies up my wrongdoings. No, it is me being unkind which causes harm and adds a burden to my soul. Not a permanent burden, just a weight that I bear every day. Burdens made from actions that aren't based on who I truly am, and jar with my inner self.

Not that I don't believe in mystical forces, I absolutely do. I just don't know if this is one of them. Or maybe it is. I don't know.

Anyways.

I contemplate these sins in the early hours of the morning when I cannot sleep because my brain whispers the tally of my wrongdoings back to me. I don't need a god to keep the score. I hold every mistake I have ever made deep within my own memory. I feel the weight of the pain I have inflicted, every disgusting word, every sordid deed, and any harm I have done reminds me that I'm no different than those who hurt me.

Then again, they do not agonize over their sins, so maybe I am different. I just want to be perfect. I want to be free. I want to be kind. Unfortunately, I cannot be perfect, I will make mistakes. I will say something I think is not rude, and it will, in fact, be rude. I will say something that I do not think is over the line, but it will be.

So instead of perfection, I must seek absolution, not from some divine source, but from anyone I harm, and from within. I need to understand that yes, I will harm others, even if I never want to. The best that I can do is to make it right, where I can. That I can apologize and work to be better. This calms me for the future, but what of the past?

Still, every day, I walk carrying the weight of my sins.

Each and every one.

Boundaries and the Underworld

For decades, I didn't really know what boundaries were. Sounds dangerous and toxic, right? It was. I had mine violated by friends, family, and bullies my entire life, and I learned to do the same.

You see, I was never really taught them. Any time I tried to set up privacy or say no or set some kind of way to be respected, I was ignored, argued with, gaslit, called sensitive, or they acted offended.

This doesn't excuse any of the boundaries I ever crossed. I still bear that, and the many ways I mistreated people.

I am sorry, and I wish I had known better.

When I finally started learning what boundaries were, it caused me to plummet into my own underworld, along with many other things that ferried me across the river Styx. Shadow work. The Dark Night of the Soul. Ego Rebirth [often called Ego Death, but the Ego does not die. To believe you have no Ego is your Ego playing hide and seek]. It has many names.

There I faced myself, my full self. Everything I had done. Everything I no longer turned a blind eye to, because I couldn't. I recognized each thing for what it was. Sin. Again, not in some Christian sense, though that is where I learned the word, instead in a real sense, the idea of the tallies of harm I had done. All of the sorrow, the pain, the anger, the harm, the crossed boundaries, the shame, the guilt, the full weight of my life.

I looked it all over and was unmade.

Hekate, the goddess of Boundaries, goddess of the Underworld, goddess of the Crossroads, brought me to the task. In answer, I put in the work to unlearn, to reform, to walk through the crossroads. I was made anew.

While she brought me here, I had to work to get myself out. If I had not, she said, if she did it instead of me, I would have learned nothing.

Decades of Patriarchal Christian bullshit washed away. Yes, I still remember everything they taught me. Some of their abusive and bigoted ideas bounce around in my head. I do what I can to deconstruct it every day. I still use some of the words I learned like sin...they serve a purpose*. But the rest? The unwarranted anger, the misplaced rage, the sorrow, the insecurity, the lies? I work to remove them from my mind every day.

This doesn't mean there is a clean slate or I ignore my past. This isn't some kind of Christian redemption where they confess, ignore the harm they have caused, and pretend it's all ok. No, this was a reckoning, a renewal, and a rebirth. The transformation of someone who still knows the weight of her actions, and can help to heal others and ensure that more and more people understand boundaries, toxicity, and how to be better.

Like a former drunk driver who hurt someone teaches others the dangers of drinking and driving.

Hekate is proud of me, and the work I put in. This I know. I still carry the weight. Some of my friends tell me I am too hard on myself, and that I could be a worse person. Honestly, they are correct. I am harsh towards myself. I recognize that and I can ease up on it and realize what a wonderful person I am. I can carry these reminders with me, as symbols of what not to do. I do this, not because I want to be some paladin of pious purity, but because I don't want to cause loss, grief, sorrow, anger, and pain.

I want to bring joy and love and abundance to those in my life.

In order to bring joy, I must go through the Underworld, releasing what has been done to me, realizing what I have done to others, and becoming a better, more empathetic person for it.

* It is important to note, here, that Hekate does not call these things I mention sin. I do, for brevity and drama. I am nothing if not a theatrical person. With her, the feeling is more...in between actions that bring negative consequences, lessons, burdens, trauma, and mistakes. When speaking and working and channeling deities, archetypes, spirits, ancestors, and our own unconscious and subconscious, there's a different language than English and sometimes it's difficult to put that into English words without a paragraph explaining it like right now. The language is more of a protolanguage or like the words behind words as I like to call it. With time you can more easily understand and translate it, but sometimes it will feel off or not be fully right. I went with sin for the

drama and the tie in to my childhood, but it's really less that and more harm, trauma, and actions that bring consequences, lessons, etc. That whole idea.

It is also important to note that I am not talking about light path and dark path or right-hand path and left-hand path. To me, the idea of "sin" or wrongdoing is causing harm to those who don't deserve it. If you want to hex an abuser, I will not deride or judge you. Go for it. If you want to hex someone who's kind because you like their partner? Ew. Work on yourself.

Strong

I don't want to need to be strong anymore

Clawing

I feel as though I'm buried
Six feet below a swamp
In a casket surrounded by mud
Clawing my way to the surface
Just once to see the sun
Take a breath of the air outside
Before descending to the depths
One last time.

Endless cacophony in my head

Please
I can't stop this endless cacophony in my head
I'm so tired
No more arguing with myself
No more contradiction
No more guilt
No more shame
No more negativity and what if's
So much pain
So much worry
So much doubt

I can't
I can't anymore
Please
I'm so tired

Can I just rest now

Time to walk away

I have spent so much time waiting for crushes, exes, and whomever to love me, all because I was terrified to walk away. "What if I walk away, and that's why it didn't work out? What if it's a lesson in patience, in showing I'm dedicated enough, that I am loyal? What if I leave, and they were almost about to tell me they like me, but now they won't?"

Yeah. I know. It's difficult and terrifying to walk away, and also it can cause some toxicity through people pleasing and other forms of manipulation. It's not that I wanted to ever be malicious or harmful. I just stayed around and thought that maybe, just maybe, they would love me someday.

This is not how love works.

I know that now. I also know some may protest. Some will say "you didn't try hard enough!" Some will pull the cards and tell me to hang on, and keep believing. I did. For 25 years of my life.

If you're reading this, feeling that you've done the same, don't be too hard on yourself. I understand that you may feel ashamed or guilty. Sit with that for a moment, but also don't hate yourself*. This is common with people who have spent their lives trying to get the people who are supposed to emotionally support and love them, to do so. It's a wound. I know you are not trying to be harmful either.

But I've learned it is harmful, to them and yourself. If they've already rejected you, and you're still holding on to some eventual yes, you're not respecting their autonomy. Don't hold on. They deserve to be respected, and so do you. You deserve someone who chooses you, every day. And you won't find that by staying in a situation where you are not loved in that way.

Let that Tower fall. Heal. Breathe. Cry. Do what you need to grieve and move forward.

Love shouldn't require this amount of work for it to happen. I get there are circumstances sometimes, like distance, or maybe they do like you and they're scared. Yes, relationships can take some work, but both have to want to do so—you can't just hold on, on your own. Love should not require you to hold out for someone to love you.

"What about Twin Flames, I hear about those in tarot love readings online all the time!"

Yeah, those are maybe a thing. We're not sure. What we do know, is that is not how it works for every single relationship. It works for only a select few where both parties heal, and put in effort once healed. If one doesn't, then you're just going back to a toxic ex [or they are...].

Look, aren't you tired? I know I've been, any time I've gotten myself caught up in this kind of a situation.

Choose you. Choose you right now, and walk away.

Seek out support from your community, and please, build up a community, we need more than one person to lean on. Learn to love yourself and heal that wound of needing to earn someone's love. You deserved better from those who withheld from you when you were younger, and you deserve better now. Then, maybe you will find someone who loves you for you, and doesn't make you earn it. Or maybe you won't mind anymore, now that you love yourself and have a wonderful community full of love and support. Everyone's life goes differently, and that's ok.

Love yourself, and know that I love you. You're healing and doing amazingly.

When I say hold space for guilt and shame, I want you to learn how to be resilient against them and not let them rule you—I don't want you to harm yourself emotionally. You're learning and growing, and that means that you will mess up and need to own that and heal. It doesn't mean you are unlovable or need to hate yourself.

The devil disguised as the lovers

I think they like you
Yeah, I'm sure of it
Yes, keep talking to them!!

Never let a message go by
Not even once
What would they think of you?
Disrespectful

"Can you help me?" Of course!
Why hold boundaries?
You can't be too difficult, right?
No, not if you want to be loved

Needs are too needy
Best not to have any of those
You can do anything they'd like
Be whomever they want

You'll find someone.

Someday.

Never show them your face
Behind that happy mask
Should they see how you really are
They'll shrink back in horror!

I know you're tired, dear one
But you cannot let go
Not yet, I mean, they nearly told you how they felt!
Not explicitly...I just have a hunch.

They'll come around.

Someone has to!

My advice is incorrect??
No, no, no, you must be mistaken
I give the *best* advice, dear...
Why would I hurt you?

To keep you here with me?
No, I am a part of you, can't you tell?
I am with you every step of the way
I *love* you, can't you tell?

Smirking? Of course I am, poppet
I am so happy for you
Did you see how they looked at you?
Any day now, I'm sure of it

Just keep holding on
Let me wipe the tears from your eyes
Did you hydrate properly?
I know it's tough, but you need rest

Shhhh shh shh, no protests.

Languish

They'll come around.

You'll see, and you'll feel terrible
All the times you doubted me...

Chasing? No, you're loyal.
You're showing how worthy you are
Look, here's another love reading, see?
You just need to *believe*.

You're not trusting me, poppet
I'm you, why won't you trust me?

What do you mean give up?
What do you mean take time to yourself?
DO YOU WANT TO BE ALONE FOREVER?
DO YOU WANT TO HURT LIKE YOU DID BEFORE?

Sorry, sorry, I'm sorry, shhh.

I just want to protect you.
That's all I've ever wanted
Please, keep trying, keep hoping
Look, it's another good love reading

I'm helping you, right?
Please, tell me I'm helping you
I saw how you were hurt
For decades, I watched

I'm not trying to hurt you
I don't want you to hurt, poppet, please
I just want you to be safe
This is safe, here, in fiction

No, I didn't mean fiction, it's—

No, it's not a lie, it's not a ghost, it's not a dream

Please don't stop, please
If you leave me, I have no purpose
I'm meant to protect you
Can't you see that??

Can't you see how I love you?

I just want to help you
I don't want you to hurt

You don't want to chase?
This is hurting you?
Holding onto dreams?

Oh.

I'm sorry

I didn't know.

Languish

I thought this was how to help you
After all you went through.

You're right.

We can let go
Walk away
Love ourselves.

A stringless marionette

A stringless marionette
Slumped and lifeless
A shadow of who I was before
Was I ever anything?

All I ever knew was shame
Guilt
Anxiety
A constant unending fear
That every action I take
Has dire consequences for us all

Lies whispered in my mind
By a figure lurking
A beast in the shadows
With an insidious glowing grin

A true Father of Lies
Not some fairy tale
Some mythological book
One I carry every day

"What a terrible thing you have done"
"You should be ashamed"
"You need to be perfect"
"Crying? You know others have it worse, right?"

Every whisper, another slice

Languish

Until I fall
My strings cut
A stringless marionette

Spirituality doesn't allow me to ignore my pain

I know this is a book about healing and love and loss and loneliness. I know that, and yet I keep interjecting things about spirituality and witchcraft. That's for a reason. Learning more about Autism and therapy, alongside of spirituality and witchcraft, are how I am learning to be a more grounded, balanced, and confident individual. All without having to mask my behaviors, judge myself, or gaslight myself. Sometimes, that's difficult–we have so much programming that teaches us all to do just that.

Having had so many wounds around neglect and abandonment, it's easy to start looking at the main characters and wanting to be them. "I will save myself and the world, and be loved and adored by many." It's a way to escape reality, where I am made to feel less than. I'm overlooked, I have difficulties with a lot of things, I have support needs, and society doesn't like that. It's a coping mechanism, and I used to feel ashamed about it. I don't anymore. I know I can be important on a small scale, and can do so more realistically than some grand tale or adventure.

That's the thing about heroes–most of us can be on a small scale, but will not have the reach or power on a grand scale. Yes, we are all uniquely us and deserve to have good things, and we can never avoid mediocre, bad or boring things. Vacations and weekends end.

Relationships end. People die. And this all hurts.

But what hurts worse? Avoiding these things. Trying to force things to stay as they are. Pretending that unending positivity and happiness give you everything you desire. Believing that every single thing you want is how things will be.

It doesn't work like that.

We can do heroic things and help others, and yet bad things will still happen. We can hope for change, and yet things will still happen that are harmful. Should we give up? No. Progress over perfection, yet again. For so long, I used my spirituality and imagination to create a world that was kind and positive, but that doesn't exist. What does, is a difficult world, where we can help others, build greater things, and also know that that is challenging. It will not go perfectly. We're not some hero in a story, where it just always goes well. We're humans.

Then again, those stories have conflict too. They can teach us that we can do amazing things. We should look to see what *we* want our story to be, not what we are told is successful or best. We also need to recognize that it's not always going to go well, and sometimes, that means we should let something go.

If I've learned anything about loss and loneliness, it's that the times I hurt the most, were when I didn't want to face a hard reality. Instead of grounding myself, feeling through it, and tending to myself and my shadow, I ignored it. I made up a different reality in my mind, and crammed all negative emotions into my unconscious. I sought signs that weren't there. I found mixed signals were actually quite clear, only I didn't think so. I re-traumatized myself. What, then, does someone do when deep in their trauma? Lash out, isolate, run away, people please, anything but deal with what's happening.

I don't blame anyone for that. Our minds have whole systems to deal with trauma that cause people to fight and lash out, run away, freeze up, stop whatever they're doing, stop communicating, and do what they can to make the aggressor and others happy through people pleasing, or isolation. These are normal responses. To me, they're not something to shame yourself for. We can learn to redirect these things into healthier defenses and coping mechanisms, but that takes time and effort. We can only do the best with what we have right now. We should never expect ourselves to be perfect.

All that said, when you are not in a trauma response, and are safe, you need to sit with the uncomfortable truths. Ground yourself and face reality. What is the alternative? You avoid it and eventually, the Tower from tarot comes crashing down* and hits you harder than if you just accepted reality from the start.

Spirituality is a way to heal. It is a way to safely face difficult and painful truths and wounds—not avoid them by bypassing them with cute sayings.

* *The Tower is not always bad, in fact even in the "bad ones", it is a removal of "bad" or rather unnecessary, painful, or unaligned that leads to "better", or necessary, healing, aligned. This alignment isn't*

something about some other dimension, at least not to me, and more of the direction of your own soul towards the life you truly want. If you want to be an author—cough, cough—you can't do that without writing. Writing is in alignment. So it's about getting on track to where you truly want to be. It hurts, so we think it's bad, but really it's chaos that leads to better. That can be cleansing, or maybe kinder, like a gift given to us that changes things for the better.

Infection

Shadow work and therapy and reflection and prose
Drawing pus from a festering wound
Who knew a heart and soul could be so infected?

Red lines of rage and bitterness and sour sadness
Stretch outward throughout the pain
Leading back to the wounds needing to be cleaned

Every tear burns like peroxide
Removing every bit of disease
How painful healing can be

Take care of those bandages
Clean your wound daily
Lest it get infected again

What an addiction it is
To pick at the scabs and cry some more
Over the things you've already healed

Hurt yourself, poke that wound more
You need more healing, right?
This is totally good for you, it's fine

Scratching and rubbing and poking and bruising
Crying as I rend my own scabs

THERE'S MORE TO HEAL

I NEED TO HEAL
PLEASE I NEED TO HEAL

Leave it alone
Let it heal
Stop scratching

Trust that it will heal

I have no energy left

I have no energy left
A lighthouse in the middle of the sea
Nothing but water for miles
Waves crashing and surging over me
The light went out long ago

I don't know that I've ever been this low
I feel listless
Time is meaningless now
All there is is anxiety
And isolation

All work and no play and all that

Shut in my home due to winter and sickness
The winter night, oppressive, long, and bleak
The sunlight and warmth, brief
Everything is either white, grey, or dark

Yet I work on myself
Hammering the metal of my own soul
To shape and restore it to glory

Again the hammer rings
I let go of an old love

Again the hammer rings
I let go of my need to escape my pain

Again the hammer rings
I let go of my fear to fail

Again the hammer rings
I let go of my need for validation

I cool the blade in the nearby water
Time for rest
There is more to be done
Another day
When I am no longer weary

All I can do is live

The silence brought by a hush of snow
That first time you hear birds in spring
Cicadas, crying out at the height of summer
Hot soup on a crisp fall day
Thunder rattling windows, coupled with the melodic sweet smelling rain
Breezes carrying the smells of the woods and fields

And then silence

I will never experience it again

I'm terrified

What good is terror though?
It does not stop what is inevitable
Nor will it slow it down
Or help me feel better
All I can do is live as fully as I please
While committing to my crafts and fellowships and beliefs
Experience as much as I can

Before it is gone

Have you tried to imagine what it is to not imagine?
To think of what it is to never think again?
Do you remember from before your first memory
or the moments in between dreams while sleeping?

Of course not, it is impossible
It twists the mind and skirts toward madness
And yet to never contemplate these things
To never understand that death is coming
Is to live on autopilot
And never truly live

A great paradox
To live
One must ponder death
One must experience minor deaths
Again and again
An end of a friendship
Graduation
Losing a job
Everything must end sometime
And yet each ending breathes new life
We die and die and die, each time reborn anew

Will it be like that too?
Or the nothing between dreams

I'm terrified

I cannot stop it

I accept it

All I can do is live

What is love to me?

I've been asking this question a lot lately. I have spent decades being taught that love is between a cisgender heterosexual man and a cisgender heterosexual woman and that's it. Between Christianity, and almost every bit of media on love, like Rom-Coms, tv shows, and princess movies, it was further reinforced. It's a man and a woman, and it has to be difficult. It starts with banter and tension, before they both realize they love each other within 90 minutes. It all wraps up with them leaving into the distance, looking into each other's eyes, or most likely, a marriage. All with some triumphant singing or piano playing music on the soundtrack for the ending.

Sometimes there's a Filofax or a poisoned apple or a castle full of books or a bass guitar involved.

I have spent so much of my life hoping to get married. I wanted to walk down that aisle and be adored. Have it be something beautiful and momentous. I wanted someone to love me for the rest of my life. I still feel that about the event, but I don't know if I want to be married. I don't even know if I want a hand fasting ceremony. Marriage can be terrible, and it can be wonderful—it came from an oppressive institution to exchange women between father and husband. It's changed for many to be more, though some still treat it that way—especially in the church. "Wives, submit yourselves to your own husbands as you do to the Lord. For the husband is the head of the wife as

Christ is the head of the church, his body, of which he is the Savior.", is a famous passage written by Paul in Ephesians 5:22-23. This is often quoted in weddings, as if that's super romantic and beautiful. No thanks, I do not want to submit my autonomy to another, nor they me. Collaboration between two autonomous people? Yes, please.

So I look at all of these things, and I am unsure. I'm a lesbian, I am not marrying a conservative Christian man, I don't have to be concerned about that, right? Then again, even if I don't have to worry, I'm still going to overthink it. Do I really want to marry, or am I doing it because it's expected? Is it truly what I want, or the long lasting love from someone wonderful and a fantastic party? Hell, if it isn't a wedding, that party will be cheaper, which means an open bar. Totally healthy idea, right?

Part of me does want a wedding and a marriage. Another part of me feels it's impractical—not for others, but for me. It feels like a silly dream. That's probably my old pain talking.

It's more than that though, too. I want to cherish and not possess, and I want to be cherished and not possessed. I want to share my life with someone, maybe more than one someone, maybe in many ways and types of relationships that don't need to be any particular way. No expectations. No relationship escalator from banter to marriage, just being, sharing, boundaries, communication, and vulnerability. Whatever feels right between us at that moment.

I don't know how that works. I've been programmed

another way my whole life, and now? Now, I feel like I'm getting this software update. I am realizing, "Oh wow, there are so many other ways to love." I want to explore all and soak them up and savor every wonderful way that I can relate with others.

I just don't know how it works and I'm slowly learning. That's ok. We all get where we need to go eventually.

Right now, I am working on communication, vulnerability, and boundaries. I can say it has been awkward and challenging–full of mistakes. I've said and done some stupid shit, to say the least. I am trying to be open about my emotions without being manipulative and immature. I am setting boundaries, and learning how to be assertive without being passive or aggressive. I have spent years being closed off while also being a people pleaser, so it is a struggle. This doesn't mean I want to let it get me down, blame others, or wallow in my own self-pity. It just is.

This is not to say that this is how all relationships should be. I don't know how anyone else's should be, other than the communication, boundaries, and vulnerability. That's key for every kind of relationship. I just feel this is what I'm working through for myself, and those that I relate with in whatever ways in the future.

All of this is happening while I'm so worn down. I feel like I've been clawing my way back to my real self after being pushed into boxes my whole life. I feel like I have all of this pain from past relationships that I'm still releasing and healing. I feel like I have these insecurities from decades of insecure relationships.

Languish

While this is difficult, I am keeping at it. I know this will not always be how it is. I want to heal, love and be.

Is this flirting?

Let's be painfully clear, as if I haven't done so in this book already–I don't know how to flirt, nor do I often know when someone *is* flirting.

Are they flirting or nice? Are they attracted to me or like my outfit? Are they smiling because they're kind? Oh, I'm attracted to them, what do I do? Do I tell them? Do I say something funny? Do I touch their arm? Oh no, is that too much? Am I crossing boundaries?? Am I being creepy? I don't want to be creepy, I just want to flirt.

I like the feeling when I know that someone else and I are flirting. I like feeling desired and sexy. I like banter and witty conversation. I like compliments and interest. I like sensuality and closeness. I like sex. I like talking about sex even without it being sexy or meaning anything other than a conversation, as long as people want to talk about it*.

Tangent aside, sometimes, my desire came from a place of trauma. I was so often ignored and overlooked, that I just wanted to be liked. I didn't mind if I was being insecure, if I was projecting those insecurities, or if I people pleased. There were times that I would be this loud and obnoxious person as if that was flirty. Other times, I would just people please and do whatever for them and not have any boundaries. Many more times, I just didn't know because I couldn't pick up on someone's motives regarding how they felt about me. It was all a bit unhealthy.

Lately, I need to know them more personally, and that

it is ok for me to flirt with them, and then I can because I feel less anxious.

I don't know.

I know I'm overcomplicating it. I know I'm overthinking it. I know that I can be flirty and not harmful. I'm letting go of a lot of my anxiety and old patterns of thought from Christianity and conservativism. I'm learning my ways of showing affection and desire, now. Sometimes I am still an idiot or aloof or awkward or say something stupid. I probably do that a lot. As much as I know things, I know pretty much nothing about charm or flirting.

I'm learning to be ok with that too.

Maybe I don't need to do anything, maybe I can just be myself, share how I feel, not be ridiculous about it, be embarrassed and regretful and own up to it in the inevitable moment that I have put my foot in my mouth.

* Too often, certain groups act like it's terrible to want physical intimacy and flirtation. They act like normal human emotions and needs are sinful and evil. Fuck that. As long as no one is harmed, as long as everyone is consenting, and as long as boundaries are respected, why should it be treated as some wicked thing? Also, no one has to like flirting or sex or talking about sex at all, there are plenty of asexual baddies out there. Some like some of it, some like none of it, some like flirting and sensuality but not sex, there's an entire spectrum of asexuality. Weirdly, somehow, the

group that tells us that sex is somehow this terrible thing unless in a very specific relationship, also says that asexuality is wrong. Like, ok, which is it, pastor?? They literally only allow you to be in a cisgender, heterosexual, and allosexual relationship. Allosexual means that you are not asexual. So to summarize this tangent, asexual people are cool. Not liking sex is cool. Liking sex is cool. Liking consent and boundaries is cool. Judging others for sex, liking sex, or talking about sex, is not cool.

The painful but necessary realization

I deserve to be loved in the ways I never was, and I owe it to myself to be that person, and ensure that I surround myself with people who love me like that as well.

I miss me

Sometimes I catch myself wanting to heal in order to find love and like then I feel like I'm just healing not for me, but for someone else. Some person I don't even know yet.

I miss me.

I miss loving myself.

I miss doing things for me, and not to feel I'm worthy.

I miss doing things for me, and not to feel like I could survive better.

I miss doing what I love.

I miss expressing love to everyone and just existing as this kind, loving person, who still holds firm boundaries.

I really fucking miss me.

I hope I return to myself for good this time.

Not a saint...not a sinner either

It's all too easy to think of yourself as this terrible person when that's what people have told you for 25 years of your life. Whether they're upset at your emotions as a child or yelling about how you deserve hell for the things you've done, you internalize all of that violent anger towards you for existing. Somehow I deserve eternal damnation for a mean word I said on the playground because I was mad at someone else. **THE AUDACITY**. It's clear, I'm terrible, and I should be tortured for it. I don't know how that sounds like a healthy philosophical idea, and yet some people keep acting like it's the best idea ever.

For 35 years, hell wasn't some other plane of existence, it was the anxiety that reinforced what was abused into me by the church, by family, and by people I thought were friends. It wasn't some land ruled by a red man with a tail and horns, it was the people around me bullying me into conformity *or else*.

It's abusive. That's really what it is. It is coercion. Discipline means "to teach", and yet no one in that group teaches. They tell you what to do and how to think *their way*. Anything else? Threats of eternal punishments. Threats of physical violence. Threats of being cast out from the only people you know. Sometimes? Very real physical violence, and being actually cast out.

Do you know what else that sounds like, other than abuse? Cult behavior.

Sometimes it takes me a bit to calm down after a panic

attack, driven by the idea that I am this wicked thing. By existing, all I do is bring pain. Of course, this feeds into so many other insecurities and issues with communicating, because I assume I'm the one who's done wrong. I'm this terrible person, and they shouldn't keep me around. Why would they?

I really hope you don't feel the same about yourself. You have kept yourself so low because of how people continuously treated you and it was unfair. I know it was unfair to me.

Here are some things you can remind yourself that while you should hold yourself accountable, you're not someone who deserves nothing but punishment.

I'm not evil, I do not enjoy when I'm harmful. I own up to it, learn from it, and try to be better.

I do not deserve punishment for existing.

I am not worthy of abandonment for making mistakes. Yes, sometimes people leave because they need to, just as I have left others because I needed a safer environment, but I don't deserve to be alone, to be hated for existing or making mistakes.

I forgive others' mistakes, so I can forgive myself.

I love others who have fucked up and made amends, so I too can be loved after making amends.

I can be kind to myself when I make mistakes. So what if I have to turn around after I just got to work when I realized I left my bag at home? It's ok, I can fix that, that isn't something to belittle myself over.

I deserve to let go of all of the self-hatred, the negativity, the self-loathing, the harsh criticisms, the emotional abuse, the internal gaslighting, all of it. None of it was mine to bear. It wasn't fair to have those I trusted as a child put all of that on me.

I make mistakes, I learn, and I do better.

I am not a saint. I am also not a sinner.

I'm just me.

Hopefully, these help you, as they help me sometimes when I expect myself to be perfect.

Finding my own security and confidence

Most days now, I have this sense of self that feels secure, capable, centered, and loved through friendships and my own love. Some days, though, not so much. Luckily, I know that healing is not linear. It feels more like a spiral to me, like the ancient idea of a labyrinth. Not the maze, a unicursal labyrinth where there is only one path that goes throughout a space in a spiral or some other shape.

As I walk, I see the same view again and again. It feels more familiar, less uncertain, and more healed each time until I reach the center.

It helps because I can remind myself that this is temporary. I can reinforce what I've learned. It feels like I am returning to myself as I traverse the labyrinth, but sometimes it can be a lot. I feel I am constantly looking over all of my long held beliefs, to see if they even fit anymore.

As I've said before, I don't know how I feel about marriage for myself. Maybe it will still be right, with the right person, at the right time. I just don't know that I want to seek it anymore. I'm not opposed, I just feel like making that goal means I will focus on a destination and worry about it. It becomes this thing in my mind that if I don't have it, then I'm not enough. If it doesn't happen, then I've failed. If a relationship isn't moving towards that, then it's a bad relationship. Is it though? Of course not. It's just become this measure of success that I'm comparing myself against and like who cares? I have added all of this pressure to it, instead of enjoying how things are. If I have needs or boundaries, if I want something more or less, I can communicate those, right?

Probably.

In the same way, even a romantic relationship feels like the same problem. It will not help me be secure, I've tried that. I was in a relationship and was an insecure, jealous, terrified mess. I expected they would hurt me, they would leave me, or would cheat. Some did, and some didn't. In all of those relationships, I was thinking about a future that wasn't, over the present that was. I made the relationship out to be more than it was. They were significant—it's not that they were not—it's that I was moving them along that relationship escalator so quickly. I felt that if I did, then I would feel safe. I never did.

I felt so much for them, a deep caring and love, but it was marred by my wounds. There was this constant need for security, and I had to be reassured a lot. I don't know, maybe I felt insecure because the relationships were and I could feel it. Maybe it was just my abandonment trauma.

Now I don't even know if I want a relationship anymore. On some levels, I do, that feeling is still sometimes there as I walk through the labyrinth, and yet other times, I'm really seeking myself. Trying to feel good and love myself. I could probably do both, though I feel terrified that I will just repeat the same mistakes.

Unhealed people deserve love too, as long as you're

willing to learn, heal, and be better. At the same time, I also know that not everyone can hold that space for someone to heal in a relationship. Plus, again, you need to at least be meeting them halfway. You need to want to heal, to respect boundaries and needs, and to be working on forming and holding your own. You need an understanding of what healthy even looks like, even if you're still healing, I think? I don't know, I'm not an expert. These are the inner ramblings I have as I unravel myself here.

I think, at least, you have to want something healthy. You have to want to try. You have to put in the effort. For me, that looks like recognizing that I am a lot more confident and self-assured than I ever was, and I'm celebrating that. It also looks like seeing where I can build more security in myself so that I'm not being unkind* to the people I love.

I feel like I'm so much closer to that center of the labyrinth. I'm closer to feeling secure enough in myself that I can move through life how I see fit. I can be present and love relationships as they are without some end goal in mind.

I can just be me, and be loved as I am. I can know that if people can't handle who I am—provided I'm respecting them too of course—then that's not my fault. That's not due to my worth. My worth still stands, even with their judgment.

One turn of the labyrinth at a time, I suppose.

*Kindness is not being nice. It still has boundaries, it still has needs, *and it still communicates honestly. Sure, sometimes we might hide things or lie for kindness too. I don't know, people seem to say that. I try not to, but I might word things more kindly while being honest. Most politeness or niceness is about protecting fragile egos, while kindness is about empathy, autonomy, and truth. Remember, we all carry our own truth, yours is not the only one.*

Are you happy?

Are you happy?

What?

Are you happy now?

What do you mean?

You know, with all of uhhhh this?

Transition?

Yeah

Yeah, I mean, happy enough, right? Like I didn't transition to be happy, I transitioned because this is who I always was, I just didn't always see it.

That's a lot to do to not be happy.

I didn't say I wasn't happy, I'm saying that my happiness wasn't necessarily dependent upon transition, just like it isn't dependent upon love and closeness and success but like my quality of life is a million times better so I'm happier overall, right? It's just not done to "be happy", it's done to "be me".

Ohhhh ok, that makes sense.

Languish

Besides, what the fuck is our obsession with happiness? Happiness, like everything else, is fleeting and diminishes. People ask are you happy, are you well? As if we're supposed to be these weird automatons with our faces twisted in permanent smiles. Sometimes I'm happy, other times I'm angry, hungry, or horny. Sometimes I want to be alone and not perceived. Sometimes I want to take the spotlight and be adored. Like life isn't so simple to be just about constant success and happiness and yet we just ignore so much of our humanity because of what? Ads? Shitty self-help? Fucking purity culture? Unnecessary politeness? It's just a weird question to answer like yeah, overall, I trend more and more towards happiness but even if I'm sad sometimes that doesn't mean my life is meaningless or immoral. I mean what the fuck is happiness?

I'm not sure. A cheeseburger?

Yeah, that works for me.

A hand darts out

A hand darts out of the cold placid lake
To draw me to its unseen breathless depths
I claw at the dock as the hand pulls me down
Whispers of my damnation on the crisp fall air
Before I slip below the surface

"You're here because you can't stop breaking your own heart. You keep loving an ideal, clinging to something that doesn't exist, doing anything to earn love. It doesn't work, does it? And the pain, does that feel good? You fail to see all the love around you, just chasing and chasing and chasing after some idyllic love. Well, you can't chase anymore. Not now. This is what you pay for your own cruelty to yourself. Cruelty must always be paid."

I look into the water, at my own face
Twisted into a sardonic smile.

"Time to pay."

I pull myself deeper and become one with the cold.

Am I dead?

What if I didn't make it
Sixteen years ago
When I rolled my car half a dozen times
Destroying part of a farmer's field at 65 miles an hour
With a start, I wake from the dream I was having
After falling asleep at the wheel
The horizon rolls before my eyes while I'm dazed
Before the wheels slam onto the ground
I get out and run, screaming, panicking
Lucky to be found by two off-duty EMTs–
Unless I died that day and I've been in hell since

Wait, no, that doesn't track
I suffered a lot throughout my life

Maybe it was the day I had a seizure
Fast asleep when I was five
I flew off the couch
Slamming into an oak coffee table
Tumbling to the floor, having hit my head many times
Dying in the ambulance ride to the hospital
Though I was a child,
Perhaps I was terrible enough before then
In the few years before death, to warrant all of this
Or maybe I had done terrible things in a former life.

I know I'm not dead.

I know this isn't hell.

Suffering just happens, sometimes a lot.

Tomorrow I will dance in my kitchen to lively music
Doing the dishes and singling along to the lyrics
Messaging the wonderful people in my life
Laughing about whatever we say

But sometimes—life feels punishing
Especially when the old wounds fester again.

6
Loving Myself

Caelynn Margaret Harper

Love yourself.
If you can't love yourself in the dark moments when you have no one else around, who will?

Walking away

I think one of the most painful reasons to have to walk away from someone is that you know that the two of you are just on different pages. You wake up one day and you realize that it's just not working. The friendship, situationship, relationship, and family, has to end.

You agonize over how to bring it up. You go back and forth on how to talk to them about why it's ending. You could even love them so much and yet you know that how it is, right now, is not working. It is causing more grief than something like this should.

The history, the way it once was, the way you wish it could be, how you feel about them, all compounding that pain. Yet you know you have to do it, for your own mental health, and maybe even theirs. I've learned this the hard way. There were times I didn't walk away. There were times I fought for relationships that had been over longer than I knew. I can tell you now, it will hurt walking away, but it will hurt less now than later.

The slow life

I cannot stress it enough, a slow life is wonderful.

Those quiet moments, where it is peaceful, and nothing much happens can be the best parts of life. I have nowhere to rush off to. Washing dishes, copying recipes from my grandmother's old index cards, making a pasta dish while listening to Italian and Parisian cafe music, hiking through the woods, and drinking at a picnic table by the lake on a hot day.

I can just be.

We spend so much time, giving our lives up to being busy. We race to make others crazy amounts of money. We run around doing things that we feel we ought to do, rather than what we want.

To a certain extent, it's necessary. Bills have to be paid, at least while the current system remains before it either eats itself into destruction, or we replace it with something more slow and meaningful in the moment. Thrilling can also be meaningful. Doing something intense and powerful can be meaningful. Yet we spend so much time just running through life to goals and not just being.

For me, that was due to anxiety. Fear of being alone my entire life. Fear of dying without accomplishing anything or being loved. Fear of leaving nothing behind and being forgotten. Fear of being unable to pay bills. Fear that if I don't have enough money, I might be evicted. All of it was fear based.

All perfectly human and perfectly absurd.

Of course, I will be forgotten someday. If this Earth is billions of years old, no one will remember me billions of years more. So why do I seek that out? Why not enjoy what I have and not waste my time running around for whatever life forms exist after us?

I have felt so utterly lonely throughout my life. This is common for people with Autism. Sometimes we want to be left alone. Other times, we want company, but it's too much to handle. Other times, people decide we're too much or not enough and isolate us. Even so, I have found solace and comfort in solitude.

Some days hurt, others do not. Nothing is permanent, including being alone or lonely. As such, why am I spending so much time running after company, affection, and attention? Can I not just relax and know that people will be there? It is human to desire company, to have friendships, to have romance, and also human to not want those things. Yet I put them to the forefront because of the pain I've carried being neglected, being left alone as a child for large periods of time.

So now I must learn that crucial balance between wanting to be around other people, and also being alone sometimes. I must learn what it is to be in a community that I can count on while being my own person too.

I have accomplished wonderful things to me in my own life. I have dreams and ambitions. I desire a full and beautiful life, not just one where I'm driven. I want quiet moments, not just working, dreaming, and trying to have notable accomplishments.

I dream of bonfires, laughter, mushy peas with a runny egg on toast and buying flowers for myself. I wish to give wonderful gifts to those I love. I desire salt and vinegar chips, cheap wine, hangover remedies, and a perfectly cooked steak. Give me medicinal plants, cute sandwiches at a foreign cafe, and the crunch of sand and gravel on a forest trail.

I do not dream of spreadsheets, promotions, or stocks. All of this is fine and good, but don't you want to just do nothing for a few days? A month? The rest of your life? Of course, it's not nothing. Just...nothing corporate. Nothing office based. Nothing like a 4-hour mandatory meeting unless that meeting is around a gaming table.

Personally? I'm burnt out. I cannot think of walking into a corporate office right now. Maybe never again. Everything I did was for someone else to make lots of money, and for me to be stressed all the time.

Now? I have a much simpler motto. Wherever I can, seek rest, joy, and the slow life.*

* This is, of course, not something everyone can do–just quit their job. I went into programming and was fortunate that I found jobs that paid well. I am grateful, and I also have emptied my retirement and accrued debt to do this. Not everyone has that, it was privilege. Again, there are bills, jobs that pay like shit, ridiculous rent prices, price gouging disguised as "inflation", you name it. Where you can, carve out time for yourself, work with friends and family and

Loving Myself

community for mutual aid, for slowness, for joy, and for revolution and liberation because we all deserve a life we feel is worth living, not just some eternal fucking slog to make investors and executives rich while the working class scrapes by due to corporate greed.

Showing myself actual care

I have spent my entire life doing what others wanted, being who others wished I would be. I stopped loving myself. I was not honoring my intuition, my body, and my emotions. I didn't even honor when I needed rest. I would burn myself out doing things for others. If I took a day to watch my favorite show or read a good book?

Guilt. Huge amounts of guilt. I felt I was wasting my life like it would pass me by. And yet, by not honoring who I am and what I wanted, my fear was coming true. I was passing myself by, living a life that I didn't want.

Now?

I'm going to go nap because I need one. I'm a bit sad and tired, and I know this is what my body and my soul need. I have spent too long making others happy. I will wear what brings me joy. I will play games, read books, and do things that inspire, heal, and bring happiness. I will spend less of my life doing what others want. I will invest my time and effort into myself, my home, and my relationships. I will go to therapy, self-reflect, and do the difficult work to heal. I will do my chores to make sure my life is slightly less messy on my own terms. I will no longer shame myself for how things are going, and instead, give myself kindness.

I will eat what I want, smoke what I want, drink what I want, and live as I see fit. I don't need unwarranted advice. I don't need other people's ego to tell me what to do with my own life and body. Nor do I want it. The funny thing is, the people who offer that advice are always the ones who don't want it either. I pray to all the gods and goddesses that no one ever tells me "I told you so," as if they're the fucking authority in my life. So what if it didn't work out? I choose what I do and do not do. Not you. The audacity and ego to judge others for what they do if what they're doing isn't harmful.

Just because something works best for you, doesn't mean you are the expert. Just because you have a specific way of life doesn't make you the expert. Just because you have a specific opinion on how things should be done, does not make you the expert. Especially in someone else's life--you are only the expert in your own.

Shut up. Let people live as they do. As for societal expectations and what work demands of us? I will do enough to earn my keep and that's it. My life is not for others' profit. Now. I'm going to go back to doing what I enjoy.

Reciprocity

I have this fear of communicating my needs. It is a shame that if I desire anything, I'm too much. So instead it bubbles up as resentment, anger, and control because that is what I was consciously and unconsciously taught to do. But if I continue this, I'm going to lose more people.

I need to be vulnerable, communicative, and honest about my needs and emotions and boundaries. Otherwise, I will grow to resent people or push them away. I need to find a way to be more open and trusting, while not letting people walk all over me.

I don't want to lose the people I have in my life right now. But if I lose people due to boundaries, or needs, or needing space sometimes to just breathe and think, am I really at fault? If I ask that we both talk more, and they say I am too needy, am I really to blame? If I say do not treat me like that, and they call me sensitive, am I the problem? If I stop talking for a day or so because I needed rest and peace and quiet from everything, did I push them away? If someone walks away because they can't handle "how weird I am" for just being my Autistic self, is that truly something I need to work on? Maybe they're not at fault either, sometimes, people just don't work well together, once the masks fall off.

Which...sucks. It just does. I understand, and it's also painful. All I want is to be accepted for who I am, cared for, and respected. When that doesn't happen, it hurts. I feel exhausted, just trying to make others happy. Even if I have

to lose others to gain my own happiness, my own sanity, and my own energy, then so be it.
    And if I have to cry to release the pain...so be it too.

Wrath

Don't incur their wrath
Keep the peace
Take down your walls
Do everything they want
Please don't make it worse
Let them be, don't call them out
It makes you more of a victim

Really?

That's your idea to reduce pain? Suffering? Trauma?

Don't poke the bear?

I will DESTROY that bear.
I don't give a fuck anymore.
I will not be told I must set MYSELF aside for them.

I am not an inconvenience.
They think so because they are weak and afraid.
I am strength
I am courage
I am not the victim–
I am the reckoning.

I will not back down anymore
When I do not agree
When they harm others

Loving Myself

When they *try* to harm me

I will not be quiet or small for anyone ever again.

Find a few things you love about yourself

I hated my body once I hit puberty. I didn't understand what was going on, and, I just felt lost. I didn't feel I fit in with the other guys, and they weren't the most reassuring about that either. I felt adrift in my own body, helpless to what was happening. I hated the smells, the body hair, the shape, the way fat held to me, the clothes I had to wear, the arousal that came with teen hormones–all of it. All while somehow both getting along with the other guys, and also not.

I didn't feel masculine in any way, shape, or form. I thought that maybe I just didn't get it. I had to show dominance. I had to take charge. I had to prove myself. I had to listen to the shitty dating advice, the ridiculous assertions of masculinity–the performance of it all. Then, *then*, I would be a **MAN**, dammit. I had to grow a giant beard, talk in as deep of a voice as possible, and lift weights to "look like an NFL linebacker", because then, *then*, I would be a **MAN**, dammit. All the while my body was increasingly foreign to me, and I didn't like how it all *felt*. Some of that was Autism and yet much of it was this sense that these parts of my body felt...additional. Unnecessary. Incorrect.

I just didn't have the words for that for decades of my life. I wasn't one of those people who knew their gender at 4 or 5. I was someone for whom gender didn't exist until puberty hit. Part of that was because of repressed feelings from Christianity, and part of it was that before my body changed, gender meant nothing. Once it started changing, gods, I wanted it to end. All of it. Even my own life.

I remember a time before I realized what was going on, and I said I hated how I looked. My friend Sam told me, "Every day, I want you to find a few things that you love about yourself." It was great advice, once I knew that I was transgender. Before I knew it, I couldn't find anything that I loved with my body. I only loved my personality traits and the things I masked with. "I love my beard (because people like it and it makes me feel like I blend in better)". Even so, when I was dating one of my exes, I shaved my beard, only to fall in love with the smoothness of my own face.

"Well, a shaved beard isn't enough to tell, I mean lots of men shave their beards!" Of course. It wasn't one thing, that's the point, it was a lifetime of things, big and small, crying out to be noticed.

There were so many times I mimicked my women friends. I was jealous of all the cute things they got to wear, while I was stuck with slabs of fabric. To be fair, there are so many fashionable items of clothing for men, but to me, it was drab, dull, and boring. Everything except for ties, I loved ties and how fun and colorful they could be. I loved scarves, pocket squares, and jewelry, but, in my mind, you couldn't wear a lot of that as a man. Thoughts that now I know are a patriarchal understanding of masculinity.

Eventually, I realized what was going on. After I started unpacking toxic ideas of masculinity, I just didn't connect with anything that had to do with being a man. I have talked about how I figured it all out. As I transitioned, I remembered what Sam said, and I began to talk about myself in much better ways. I love how my hair looks today. I love how this dress fits me and complements me. I love how happy I look every day. I love how I can finally see myself every day that I look in the mirror.

Also, I have a nice ass. You know, whatever works.

Finally being able to love myself and my body was so beautiful. It wasn't always easy, some days, I couldn't even find one thing to love, even after starting to transition. But eventually, I connected more and more to my body. I had a deeper sense of self. I loved all the wonderful parts of me, perfect or imperfect.

There are still things I know I will change about myself. Loving and accepting myself does not mean that I have to stay the same for the rest of my life. There are still things that stress and hurt me, and I know I can change that. I don't have to hold onto them and pretend to be okay. I don't have to follow what people think on how I should or should not accept myself, transition, whatever. It is my life, my body, and I will do what I know is best for me.

Transphobic people scream that I just need to accept my body as it is and be "gender non-conforming"*. Fuck them. They don't understand, and if they do, then they're probably denying parts of themselves that are screaming out like me. Not all of them, mind you—some people are hateful for other reasons than projecting their denial. Regardless, I can transition how I see fit, all the while thankful for the beautiful advice from my dear friend Sam.

I can be grateful for how it has helped me love my body, even if some things need to change.

I love my body, and only I get a say on the matter.

** The people who yell about how I should be a gender non-conforming man who wears feminine clothes but is still a man, are the same people who yell about Harry Styles and other men doing **exactly that**. They don't care. It's not about protecting women, or us from ourselves, it's about controlling what others do in their own bodies, and is another form of the patriarchy that they swear up and down they are against, while upholding it against everyone, including cisgender women, in their arguments, ideals, and tweets.*

Self love

Every time I am told to love myself before others can love me, it breaks my heart. In my mind, I do love myself. I care about myself, all I have is me, and I have to be alone until I am perfect? That feels like too much pressure.

I see this discourse around being perfect to be loved, but no one says that *outright*, of course. That would be clearly cruel. Instead, they hide it behind "reason". You can't be needy. You can't show interest too soon. You have to rid yourself of codependency. You have to be perfectly happy on your own. Meanwhile, others say you don't have to be perfect to be loved. You don't have to be hyper-independent, and instead, come from a place of boundaries and interdependence. That you're allowed to have needs and communicate them. The key is finding community and love that fits that for you.

Which of those sounds better? I'd rather have community and love, rather than try to fix myself for the rest of my life.

Oddly enough, by realizing I'm worthy of love, needs, and boundaries, I am, in fact, loving myself before I love someone else. It's just that that phrase means something completely different than what our hyper individualistic society wants. It means something completely different than how people use it.

I get we want to have a strong sense of self, but that doesn't happen as someone who isolated themselves. Take it from me, I have isolated myself a lot. It is really difficult and painful to be so alone. There are so many poems in this book, about that. It's not that I need this perfect sense of self without anyone else ever, no.

I'm allowed love while I heal. As for boundaries? They are of course important to protect against shitty people. As for needs? They are important to communicate because we all have needs, every one of us.

Is that "loving yourself before you can have love"? I don't know, I don't think so. I prefer the idea that we can heal while being loved. We can mess up, make it right, and still be loved. It's about that aftercare, rather than being perfect. Sometimes we will still lose people due to our needs and boundaries. I'd rather have that happen, and feel the full weight of it than pretend I'm perfect or that everything is fine. I'd rather be messy and grieve and be human.

That's what I want, not some idea of me being perfect and hyper-independent.

Rejection sensitive dysphoria

Rejection is morally positive. It helps us create and maintain necessary boundaries for everyone's autonomy and safety. It also allows us to communicate effectively. That does not mean it is easy to reject someone, nor is it easy to be rejected. Especially if you have rejection sensitive dysphoria, which is a part of disorders like Autism, Attention-Deficit/Hyperactivity Disorder, Borderline Personality Disorder, and other forms of anxiety and neurodivergence.

Every disagreement, every argument, every conflict, every change in someone's behavior, every failed plan, every ghosting, every full-on rejection carries with it the weight of all of them before. A million emotions swell, and for me, I have a difficult time with it sometimes. I either shutdown or meltdown, I sob, I have difficulty breathing, I feel severe pains in my chest, and in the past, I would act out or lash out. Sometimes I feel like I'm worthless. Other times I feel that I deserve all of this and that they hate me and don't want to be around me anymore. All from something that can seem so small.

Now that I understand rejection is a positive thing, I have a much easier time with it. Is it still difficult? Absolutely. Now, though, I have ways to feel through it and manage it, while making sure it is not their problem. It is mine alone. Sometimes, if I need, I can lean on my support network, like friends, family, community, and my therapist, but not them.

To help manage some of it, like the difficulties with change, I can communicate some needs, like let me know of changes as soon as possible. If something falls through and it's not indicative of issues, I can ask that people let me know. This helps me understand that it's not me, it's just a circumstance that is happening. I still have to own the weight of it.

I still deeply struggle with it.

While I'm trying to learn how to manage it, it can be frustrating. It can be difficult to communicate my needs without feeling manipulative. Years of people I trusted deeply, gaslighting my boundaries, emotions, and needs, will do that. I want to be vulnerable and assertive, but not manipulative or aggressive, and when people have gaslit you, remembering how that works is a struggle. I still have a need for security and reassurance. I just want to make sure that I'm communicating everything fairly and effectively, while watching for red flags of manipulation from others.

I'm still learning how to properly hold space for everything. I think there are ways to allow space for people with RSD to have security, while allowing others the autonomy to be able to disagree, make changes, reject ideas and people, etc. And also people don't have to help you process your feelings, right? I think it comes down to communicating in ways that help those you love to feel secure, while still speaking your truth. If they can't handle that, that's really on them.

Just like everything, there are no easy-to-follow rules. There are exceptions and a lot of nuances to everything.

There are ways for us to mitigate RSD through teaching people to be able to sit and feel through difficult emotions, and communicating more effectively. We can do so, while remembering that rejection is morally positive, and we all deserve security, which includes setting boundaries and rejecting whatever we want to.

Not feeling does not make you better

I don't understand the whole idea that emotions are bad. I understand that this idea is due to the patriarchy. I understand that it is done to remove us from our humanity and put us into a passive state. Why? Because if you feel your emotions, it becomes very clear very quickly that this whole system we live under is not working for anyone except white, cisgender, heterosexual men. Even for them, it's barely working, because it disconnects them from themselves and their truth. They let go of their own truths to gain the benefits of a malicious collective, pushing this idea that emotions are manipulative, and logic is the end all be all of honesty.

As if logic without emotions and humanity could never be harmful. As if emotions are unreasonable or illogical in situations that call for them. As if cishet [cisgender and heterosexual] men have never said "just be reasonable" or "Why can't you be logical" to shut down the very rational and emotional response to being gaslit, attacked, manipulated, talked over, or harmed.

Emotions are a part of us and happen for a reason. They tell us that something is happening, and I like to think of them as a notification system. Sometimes it's something like "oh this is a good thing, I want more of this", so we smile, laugh, and feel elated. Other times, it's something like "oh, this is dangerous", so we get angry, we disengage, and we fight our way away from something bad. It is not emotions that are bad. It is that us misusing them to harm, or us ignoring them to the point that we lash out, is bad. It is a lack of emotional intelligence and maturity that is bad, not emotions themselves.

This is why it is so ironic that certain men will shut down emotions, saying that everyone else is being emotional, while being stubborn, angry, and obstinate. As if those are not emotions. They pretend that their emotions are bad, when it is their refusal to understand their own emotions that lead to issues. They deny that emotions can be logical, and then lash out in emotion at someone expressing an actually logical idea, because they don't like the person's tone of voice. Or it isn't happy or positive.

That is not logic, that is anger. That is an irrational moment of anger, unlike someone being upset for being discriminated against, which *is* a rational form of anger. All emotions are just notifications, and I'm not judging anyone for having them. I suggest that since you are going to have them anyways, you need to understand why they bubble up, and how they are affecting your thoughts, behaviors, and actions. You're allowed to be upset and angry. You're not allowed to then treat people like shit because of it, and because you're mad that they're calling out harm.

So then, why shut down emotions? Because they point out some very important truths that often manipulative and abusive people in positions of power don't want us to know. If we are centered in our own wisdom, in our sense of self, in our logic and emotions, we are less easily controlled and manipulated. Keeping us away from our emotions, from our center, keeps us away from our truth, and stuck in cult-like followings. If you cannot feel terror over the way you are controlled, then you won't notice that it is happening. Or if someone controls and manipulates your emotions, they can hold sway over your opinions, thoughts, and actions.

It is easy to get people to side with an abuser or oppressor if you call the victim "emotional" and "not rational". It is a thought terminating sequence, that stops the conversation from continuing in a way that can actually resolve conflict and harm. To the person saying it, it is not about the fact that the person's response *is actually rational*, it's about stopping the conversation with an ad-hominem, so that it cannot continue. It is a tactic to keep the truth from being found, and to gaslight people into believing the aggressor.

Can emotions be toxic and manipulative? Absolutely. Can we be mistaken in what we feel? Yes. That is why we need to not demonize emotions, and instead teach people how to be emotionally intelligent and mature. We need to learn not to shut them down or ignore them or treat them as evil. Instead, we can learn how to feel them, process them, embody them, and communicate them.

I think another main reason we don't feel our emotions fully is because it hurts. It's terrifying. To feel through trauma is painful and frightening. To sit with the uncomfortable feeling that you've been bigoted in any other way, is painful, and embarrassing. Guilt is uncomfortable. It's also uncomfortable to remember how some of your family and friends have hurt you so deeply, or how you've hurt them.

It's a lot to process, but it is worth it. In doing so, in a healthy way, it allows us to find the wholeness of ourselves, the wholeness of our truth. It allows us to learn what our boundaries are, and how to properly set them and hold them. It allows us to learn what our needs are and how to communicate them. It allows us to determine who stays in our lives, and who goes. It allows us to heal, grow, and recognize the toxicity in ourselves and others. It allows us to unlearn our toxicity, and to be better every day.

Lastly, it allows us to find people who are connected to themselves as well. We can then build a community of people who have healthy boundaries, needs, and communication. We can work together to help each other in a system that denies us our truth.

Emotions are necessary for a full human experience, and should not be ignored, denied, or treated as less than.

Accountability

Apologies without action and change are just manipulation.

Regret is not accountability. It is really just the first stage towards it. It is the moment you recognize that what you did was harmful, but if you stay in that place, you are not actually holding yourself accountable. You are self-flagellating. Punishing yourself because you feel you deserve that, rather than doing something.

That's where I was for so long. Regret over the people whose hearts I played with. Remorse over the racism, sexism, homophobia, and transphobia that I perpetuated for so long. Wishing that I stood up for myself or others, instead of the times I said and did things that hurt people, especially while drunk. Knowing that I made people feel unwelcome, uncomfortable, or unsafe, and never wanting to make anyone feel that way ever again. Grief over not walking away when I should have. Embarrassment over drinking my pain, Autism, Gender Dysphoria, and anger away. Hiding these things, instead of healing and accepting them. Finally, annoyed over the ways I voted and the ideas I backed before I learned better.

I could go on, listing a million regrets in only a few decades, but that wouldn't help anyone if I stopped at regret. Instead, I had to heal. I had to take accountability within myself for what I had done and not shy away from it. I had to understand that I was capable of harm, of judgment, of bigotry. I had to understand that I had done these things, and not deny it. I had to own every single thing I had done.

Only then could I start to unpack and unlearn and undo it. Healing is not a comfortable process to do. It requires you to see every part of you, beautiful and grotesque, and accept that it is there. Accept who you are. Accept what you've done. Accept what others have done to you. This doesn't mean you are happy with it, you're merely saying "this is what is."

Then, you can look at "this is what will be." This is how we move forward, by healing instead of continuing cycles of harm.

Frivolity

A million frivolous crushes
Would I change any one?
Never
Let me be wistful
A million wild frontiers of love and passion and romance
Even if I know it will never be
That it is not reality
Allow me the chance to dream

Walking in shadows

One of the biggest turning points in my life was realizing that someone I loved, loved me, but it wasn't in the same way. At the very least, it wasn't going to work out. That broke me. I wept for months while also having a crush on someone else. It's safe to say that I was a mess. It wasn't loving multiple people that was the mess, I get that, as long as everyone is on the same page, like with polyamory. The mess was that I was sobbing most nights, and ignoring that I needed time to heal. All while wanting to jump right back into romance and dating.

I needed time to grieve.

I also needed to process everything that had happened over a decade. I couldn't just ignore that. I had to heal my trauma from when I was younger, and also grieve this recent loss. I needed to understand why things never really seemed to work out for long. The only way to do that was to look back over all of my relationships.

I had to allow the pain to bubble up from my subconscious and be felt, seen, and understood. This is the crux of shadow work, along with accepting ourselves fully, even if there are things we want to work on. I could have ignored it, but healing comes from letting ourselves be uncomfortable enough to look at what we've avoided. It is going to be painful, difficult, and uncomfortable. *That* is *exactly* why it is often avoided, and why it should not be.

You have to be careful when dealing with trauma,

though. Shadow work is something that can deepen your trauma if you're not giving yourself the time, the space, and the love, to work through it at a pace that doesn't completely tear open that wound. Yes, wound care will hurt, but we don't need to rub lemon juice and salt on a cut, right?

The same goes here.

We need to be honest with ourselves and feel the things we've been putting off. We must evaluate the thoughts we've denied, via holding space for our trauma and regrets, our thoughts, behaviors, and actions. And we need to love ourselves while we do. We need to care for ourselves during that time. Clean the wound. Dress the wound. Drink fluids. Rest. See a trauma informed care professional when and if needed.

This is not a time to judge ourselves. We're not doing confession to find out how we've displeased god. We're not looking for more instruction from the pastor here. What we're doing, is seeing all the obstacles in the way of a life we want to live, including obstacles within.

If you feel you cannot deal with a specific wound right now, don't. Deal with a smaller one, and come back later.

For me, one of my deepest wounds that are infected and keep causing problems is because of neglect, bullying, and abandonment. I've always felt like you have to earn love from others, especially if they didn't really show you the same amount of love back. For years, I have chased after unrequited love. I have spent eons trying to read between the lines of people's intent, which, with autism, is not easy. It's not that I always miss social cues, often I notice them, but I can't tie the intent to them. I don't know if it's friendly or flirty, if it's honesty or manipulation, if it's sarcasm because I didn't understand something, or if they're just like that. Unfortunately, I'm often wrong whenever I guess to which it is.

And that's why I'm alone. I know I have this deep, earth shattering love I'm meant to experience, I've known my whole life. It's like I came here knowing that. But I didn't know how to recognize everything, until I had done some shadow work. I needed to unpack decades of trauma, bullying, shame, guilt, and embarrassment. It was immensely painful. I still struggle with it, but it's something that I see more clearly with every new lesson I learn.

I deserve the kind of love that isn't hidden or unspoken. I deserve a love that is fully expressed. I know that now, because I've sat in that pain and felt what I was afraid to feel.

If you feel ready to do this, here are some questions to get started:

What are you afraid to feel?
What are you afraid to say?
What are you afraid to think?
What hurts you?
Who hurts you?
What do you pretend is ok, when it really isn't?

What would you change in your life if you had the power to?

Be afraid, that's ok. That's human. Don't shame yourself for that fear. Feel it. Process it. Own it. Love it. Love yourself.

Reading between the lines

Love isn't an implication or inference, it's an action. If I have to read between the lines to imagine you love me, you don't love me. I shouldn't have to read tarot to understand your feelings, you should communicate them. I shouldn't have to argue with myself over what this message meant or that gift meant, it should be stated. Maybe that sounds harsh, but I am autistic. I am already using most of my energy surviving and taking in massive amounts of sensory, emotional, and other input. I don't have the energy to spend most of my time trying to divine what you mean because you can't be straightforward with me about what you feel, or want.

People act like the unspoken is romantic, fuck that. You know what's romantic? Someone saying "I want you" and meaning it. *That* is romantic. Show me that. I would melt in a second.

I understand that sometimes that is not easy. I struggle with communication too. It's not that I want to be harsh, I'm just tired, sad, and wish things could just be clear for a change. That for once, if someone likes me, they would say it. Show it. Live it.

I don't think I'm the only one, I see people constantly wanting love readings. They are looking for advice on how to read someone's intent with them. They want to know what to expect. They want to see how they feel.

What are we doing here??

Why aren't we just saying what needs to be said to each other?

Also, if someone says they don't like you, they don't want anything like that with you, *believe them*. Walk away from that idea. If you want to be their friend, awesome, but be their friend. Did you break up with someone? Grieve it. Don't sit there and ask if they're coming back, do you really want that? I thought I did, and guess what? It was miserable. If someone keeps toying with you, don't try to read their feelings with divination. Instead, go out and find someone who won't toy with you.

Seriously, what the fuck are we doing here??

This is why I rarely like love readings, they espouse that someone is coming back, loves you, and that you should let them. Let it be so. Yet I shouldn't have to divine that, and neither should you. I would much rather we just trust that someone who cares will love us someday, than eternally wonder if someone does love and care. Why would I hold onto someone who said no, left, plays hot and cold, says they love you but they can't leave their partner, or whatever other bullshit is going on? I have seen some crazy comments on love readings. Fuck that.

I also understand that sometimes people can't be with you until they heal first. This is not that. This is when you hold out for something to work that you know just isn't working. Heal. Grieve. Respect and love yourself. Find someone who actually shows you how they feel about you.

Imagine

Imagine how happy someone will be when you show them such kindness, empathy, warmth, and love, and they reciprocate it. When they are grateful for you, and you them. When they are in love with someone they feel is so wonderful.

Realize then, that you are still that wonderful, wholesome, beautiful, passionate, empathetic person, even without them. Show yourself that love now. If someone happens to be in your life in the future, you can show them that love too.

Loving my sadness

The nice thing about finally learning to love yourself, is that you give yourself the license to be authentic at any time. You no longer hate yourself when you're sad. You no longer view sadness, anger, or anything else as some incredible moral failing.

It just exists. You feel this sadness without identifying yourself as sad. Instead, you view it as a temporary situation to feel your way through. I know that it is not permanent. This helps me release fear, anguish, pain, sorrow, and so many other difficult and powerful emotions. It also highlights what feels off or missing or painful in my life.

It is a beacon for change, and a powerful one. And sometimes, it is a reminder of how far I've come. A view into what I've lost, and what I've gained, to be who I am today.

And sometimes—it's just pain.

That is ok too.

Guidance

Sometimes I feel like I just don't know what is true. Anxiety can really mess with you. So much of my life has been untangling anxiety, autism, rejection sensitive dysphoria, and such from my actual intuition.

There are so many readings, so many teachings, so many ways, so many choices, and sometimes, it makes my head spin. I feel like a crucial part of the last few years, during this chthonic journey of mine, has been learning to hear my own intuition and trust my own guidance.

People will tell you what to do, where to live, what to wear, and get so mad when you don't listen. What they don't realize is that while that fits them, it doesn't fit everyone. Hell, half of the advice they sling is just recycled. Mine probably is too.

I don't even think many of them believe it. We're just repeating our biases over and over again. Meanwhile, we are surprised that someone has a breakdown at 50, wondering what they could have done better in life.

Learn to hear your own guidance. What brings you joy? What moves you? What makes you feel at peace? What do you fear? Why? I know that we can't all be crazy successful business people. We can't all live up to what society says we're supposed to be. We shouldn't. We should do what we need to survive, of course, but also we should do the things we love. That doesn't mean there aren't any obstacles, of course. Costs can add up and we're in an economic system that keeps nearly a hundred million

Americans living paycheck to paycheck. Where we can, though, I think it's crucial to listen to our inner guidance. This will bring in more peace, joy, and help us to move towards what we want in life.

Some things will not work out. Almost all of us will never become billionaires, and most will not become millionaires. We may not have everything we dream of to work out, and that's ok. I don't think life is about having every idea we come up with become reality. We can still have a lot of joy and fulfillment without every dream coming true. I once was engaged and thought that that was how my life would go, and it was not. Do I regret that time? Absolutely not! It was a wonderful part of my life. Might I get engaged later? Maybe, who knows! But I don't have to attach to that idea, or the idea of being a billionaire, in order to live well. I can know that some dreams will come true, and move toward what I want in life, even if some things fall through.

As for the obstacles? This is why we need community, to celebrate when things go well, to support when things do not work out, to help each other thrive, and to tear down those oppressive obstacles.

What is self-love

Love is a special interest of mine. While living this life, I feel I've been working towards understanding myself and love, and further, loving myself.

When someone asks you if you love yourself, what do you think? What does loving yourself mean to you?

To me, it used to look like pretending and using Pinterest boards full of self-care tips. Now, it looks more like listening to my emotions, body, and taking care of myself and my home. I am learning to listen more each day, especially knowing when to rest, even if I'm not always succeeding at that. I am often tired. I am reminding myself of my worthiness by just being alive, which, is difficult for me, having had a lot of people in my life make me feel worthless. I am reminding myself I am loved as often as I can, because sometimes this is difficult to believe. I am seeking joy and comfort, yes, sometimes even in that Pinterest level self care. Other times, I am seeking self-care through painful self reflection.

It isn't a pain I take on as a form of harm, but it can be painful. It can be painful to look at the difficult feelings, memories, failures, and shortcomings about yourself. It can be painful to look at the wounds others have inflicted on you, in order to show these places in your mind and heart compassion. To learn from them. To heal them. The trick is to learn from them, forgive yourself, release the difficult emotions, and move forward. It doesn't help to keep yourself stuck in a state of self-flagellation, punishing yourself as though you're a medieval monk terrified of an angry god. This one is difficult for me, as I am sometimes still terrified of the angry god I grew up with.

Healing is self-love. Especially as the way to heal is often to view these things you don't love about yourself, with love. It seems impossible at times, but if you start with something small, like "I don't like how I spoke to so-and-so" and then view it as "I am a person who sometimes makes mistakes. I know how I went wrong, and at the same time, it's ok. While it is not ok to harm others, I know that sometimes, I will. Even so, I am still worthy of love and compassion. When I make mistakes, I can apologize. I can work to restore that relationship. I can learn, grow, and be better in every moment. Even if I fail again." This becomes a bit easier each time. You might keep struggling with it from day to day. Some days are just difficult, I know that full well, and that too is ok.

Not everything that needs love in ourselves is a mistake, sometimes it's a painful memory caused by trauma or suffering. We may have adopted someone else's opinion as our own, calling ourselves stupid whenever we fail, or selfish if we set a boundary. In these moments, it is also important to challenge these ideas. It is important to remind ourselves that we are amazing and worthy of good things. If that sounds like too much, you can start at neutral. You can say "I'm a human who has needs and boundaries, and those needs and boundaries should be respected". You can work your way up from there.

Self-love isn't about being perfect, having the best routine, and constant positive affirmations. Sure, it can include some of that, but not perfection, remember, perfection is impossible. It's about showing up for ourselves. It's compassion and love for ourselves. It's showing the world, and ourselves, who we really are.

This can be about authenticity and hyping ourselves up, and also goes beyond that to protect ourselves. This includes confronting negative self-talk, recognizing when people cross boundaries, and advocating for our needs when they are not met. It's not all positive affirmations, cozy baths, and pleasant scents in candles. It can be full of conflict. People who hurt you, might not like you walking away. Hell, they'll make you the villain for "up and not talking to them anymore out of nowhere" after months, years, or decades of crossed boundaries, lack of support, disrespect, etc.

It's about remembering who we are, and being our fullest selves, without shame and guilt.

It's not about perfection, as that cannot be. Progress over perfection is a much better idea. Like anything, it compounds. The more we show up for ourselves, the more we love ourselves, the more we are authentic, the easier it becomes, and we do it more and more. It's time you started loving yourself, fully, each and every day. If you forget or fuck up, that's ok.

Progress over perfection.

Love yourself.

What if

What if you're not codependent, what if you just have abandonment trauma?

What if you're not needy, you just have needs?

What if you're not "too much", you're just too much for that person, but enough as you are?

What if you're not "not enough", you're just not enough to that person's expectations, but are perfect as you are?

What if you remembered you're a fucking badass who deserves love, and deserves to love yourself?

What if you are proud of yourself for putting yourself out there and saying what you want and need, even if someone doesn't feel the same?

What if you showed up for yourself, again and again, when others didn't?

What if you remembered how amazing you are?

What if you stopped feeling guilty for existing as you, while still checking your thoughts and behaviors for toxicity and harm, working to be kinder to yourself and others?

What if you loved yourself, showed yourself patience, and realized you're doing the best that you can right now? That you deserve to honor your needs and emotions and respect yourself? That if you made mistakes, you can learn from them so that you avoid that mistake again without shame or judgment? That people who mistreated you, did so because they were projecting their own pain, not because you deserved it? Because you didn't deserve that. At all.

And you don't deserve to continue to harm yourself as they did.

Liberation through literature

I am liberated
With every stroke of my pen
Every clack of the keys on my keyboard
The ink and cursor flow
Like the words through my mind
As I write, the storm of my thoughts begin to clear
I am a whirlwind, a torrent of emotion and creativity
Sentences cascade like rain from the clouds
Until it passes and the sun shines bright
I am at one with my own divinity now
And I feel free

When was it

When was it when I decided
That I could only receive
After I had given everything and more?

When was it when I decided
That I was not allowed good things
After all of the good I did?

When was it when I decided
That I was not good enough
After I believed everyone else was

Did I decide
Or was I taught?

Why am I not good enough?
Even without giving?
Am I not inherently human?
Not perfect but not evil?

I am growing
Learning
Healing
Renewing

I am not who I was before
Why is it so difficult
To believe that I could receive?

Loving Myself

That I am truly worthy?

I'm tired of thinking
Of feeling
Of entertaining
Any opinion from anyone
That I am not worthy
That I am not enough

Don't fuck it all up now

When you've experienced a lot of trauma and chaos, when things finally get normal, your mind *looks* for the next disaster, struggle, traumatic event, etc.

It's so used to it that it doesn't understand like "oh, we're safe now for a bit." This is why when things are quiet, you're still freaking out. You're finally holding space for all of this trauma and it is *painful*. At this time, if you know you're safe but you're still looking for shit to go sideways, you need to rest*. You need to breathe through it, and you need to remind yourself that you're safe. Things can go well. That you can handle yourself even if it *does* go sideways.

I've been freaking out for months while I'm writing this book. I've been scared of food scarcity, fascism, people I love hating me, people who I *should* trust so much more but I have a hard time due to trauma, being forced to de-transition by the government, violence from people who hate gay trans women, violence from people who hate witches...the list goes on.

I'm not saying these are impossible. They're all scarily very possible, but they're not happening right now. It's good to be prepared, but when you're consistently panicking, I think it's time to find security in yourself.

And that's not always easy. Believe me. As much as I am saying "get rest", this book is clearly a guide for me to keep reminding myself to rest. I'm right with you.

What's been helping me is finding healthy ways to

release the worry. Of course, breathing and meditation *can* help but sometimes, especially with trauma, they don't always. What then? How do I get back into now? I journal. I cry. I dance. I feel what I need to feel and write out all of my worries until I can't think of any new ones, sifting off impurities from a gorgeous emotional consommé. I try my hardest to listen to those parts of me and not judge or correct them–just listen.

Sometimes I make backup plans. Sometimes I eat comfort food. Sometimes I stim to help the autistic parts of me calm while I deal with this. I create. I do things that bring me joy. I get out in nature. I take naps. I talk to my grandparents who passed. I talk to Hekate. I learn about trauma. I seek connection. I try to understand my needs and boundaries and uphold them to give myself room to feel and experience and worry and heal.

There isn't a cure-all. It takes consistent work. I need to be consistently grounding myself, listening to my body, my thoughts, my emotions, and my intuition. Not everything works every time. I have to change it up sometimes. One, the main thing is I don't want to bottle it all up anymore. I want to hold space for this pain and fear, in order to sort out anything I need to and feel through the rest. Two, I don't want to make decisions on it unless maybe it's to make a contingency plan. Plans are helpful sometimes for easing the mind when they're not getting carried away. Three, I want to love myself and not shame myself for these things. I want to show every part of me that I am worthy of kindness and compassion and love, even when I'm terrified.

I still freak out sometimes when everything is perfectly normal, and that's ok.

I know that I am taking care of myself in the ways I need.

Remember, rest is not just sleeping. It is doing things that you enjoy, to refill your energy. It could be hiking in the woods, playing your favorite video game, trying a new restaurant, or anything that helps you relax and recuperate.

Did I ever really love myself?

If you asked me before, if I loved myself, I would say yes. I thought I did. My opinion of myself was that I loved myself, and I wanted good things, but I didn't really show myself love. I said shitty things about myself. I accepted cruel behavior from others and kept them around. I blamed myself for how others hurt me. I held onto hopes of things rather than being present. The list goes on.

Of course, I cannot be perfect, yet I can start actively loving myself. I can do so, not just by saying it or with face masks and tea, but by also setting boundaries with myself, not just others. I shouldn't say mean things about myself. I should challenge mean thoughts about myself. I shouldn't accept cruel behavior from people. I can set boundaries with them, and communicate how to respect me, and if that doesn't work? I can then see that as a red flag and walk away. I should not blame myself for the things I had no control over, that I did not cause. I should be present with how things are, not what I think things could be.

I deserve to love myself fully and mean it.

I'm the fucking Empress

I spent too long hoping people who didn't like or love me would. I spent too long hoping people who weren't attracted to me would be. To say I was being foolish would be an understatement. I do not mean that to judge myself, it's to recognize that I have a lot to learn. It was also foolish in the way that the Fool in Tarot is foolish-ready for new beginnings and leaps of faith at any given moment.

Looking back, it was clear but at the moment I would tell myself stories with tarot readings and over-analyzing everything. Yes, some people led me on. Others did like me and then left. Other times, I was too invested too soon. Or it just simply didn't work out but I clung to this idea of it working. These were all the times I had hopes for something that wasn't real because I didn't love myself enough to let go, or to see it as it was.

Fuck that, I don't want to do that anymore. I deserve to love myself enough to see things as they are. I deserve to love myself enough to see all of the love in my life. I deserve to love myself enough to be open to healthy, reciprocal, emotionally available relationships. I deserve to love myself enough to be vulnerable while not being toxic in how I express my emotions and needs. I deserve to love myself enough to be with vulnerable and communicative people. I deserve to love myself enough to be with someone who makes it clear how they feel about me. I deserve to love myself enough to surround myself with loving friendships too—all of this doesn't have to only be about romantic love. I deserve to love myself enough to not worry about my future, as I will always be there for myself.

This isn't exhaustive, but it's a start. I thought I loved myself and yet I kept hurting myself and others. No more. I know my worth now, and I know what I deserve. I also know what others deserve from me too.

I'm the fucking Empress.

What I learned from the Leo sign

Self-confidence is self-love through knowing what my worth is, and not negotiating from that.

That does not mean being uncompromising, it means holding firm boundaries, with others and yourself. It means to be honest, vulnerable, and courageous–things Leo embodies so well. It does not mean to make yourself higher than others. Rather, it means to not make them higher than you, nor you higher than them. It is a place of mutual respect, integrity, and compassion. It means letting go of arrogance, and not allowing it in others with how they treat you.

Emotions are difficult

One of the things that have made healing so difficult is how deeply Autism impacts how I feel. I think being transgender has too, but in a different way. Connecting to my body, and feeling like myself after decades of pretending to be a man, has helped me understand more of my emotions. Even so, Autism and trauma still can make it tough.

I know people will read this and go "this happens to everyone!!" Ok cool, look into being Autistic then. Or, maybe, listen to Autistic people and realize that while there are similarities, it is not the same thing. I hate that, "this is how autism affects me," is met with, "well EVERYONE goes through THAT!" Really? Do certain stores make you want to crawl up into a dark hole and cry because the lights are too bright, there's too much noise, there are too many people, the options are overwhelming, and you're not sure always what you want or need?

"Ok, I get that, that doesn't affect me like that. Well, maybe you're just highly sensitive, a starseed, an indigo child, or an empath!"

No. I am Autistic, and also spiritual. I can be both, without needing to use spirituality to bypass the very real needs and ways in which my mind works that I have from a very human and well-known condition—Autism. I used to identify with these things, I used to be like "wow, yeah, I'm definitely hypersensitive!" Of course, I am. Autism causes your senses to be hypersensitive. But it's not just hypersensitivity.

I used to think I was an Empath. Then I realized that that was caused by just having empathy, even hyper empathy due to Autism and trauma. Most people who feel like they're Empaths, even if not Autistic, most likely have trauma to heal. This alone allows them to pick up on people's changes in emotions due to hyper-vigilance. You needed it to avoid danger.

I don't know much about Indigo children, and I don't need to. I know I have Autism and that's enough for me. I've heard people mention that this is also maybe Autism or ADHD, and honestly? Probably. New Age Spirituality puts magic over the mundane, and I'd rather not. Mundane explanations first, then the magical. Sometimes it's not that someone has spiritual issues and *that's* why they react to incense–maybe they're just allergic.

I never fully identified with Starseeds. I liked some of the oracle decks, as they had some nice messages. Eventually, though, as I learned more about it, it felt like space Christianity mixed with like space racism and QAnon conspiracies. Some even talk about how the Aryan aliens came to teach us better than our former ways. Aryan aliens. And they say that these "pure light skinned beings are here to make us better." How is that *not* just Nazi ideals, wrapped in some new space religion? 5D Ascension sounds like the Rapture. Many still talk about a creator God [don't worry, he's *totally* different]. Oh, and Jesus? He's a consciousness, we can all be like him.

It gets more racist and anti-Semitic as you go. QAnon talks about lizard people ruling the earth, calling them globalists. "Globalists" and "lizard people" are well known anti-semitic dogwhistles. Guess who else says these things? You guessed it, starseeds. So needless to say, I've avoided that whole idea ever since. Even a cursory look into the history and usage of many New Age Spirituality concepts like these will dive into white supremacy, fascism, the patriarchy, colonization, anti-scientific views, spiritual bypassing, eugenics, a space opera form of Christianity, and toxic positivity. They're often a pipeline into these far-right ideologies.

This may sound outlandish, but it is not. I don't need to lie about these things to keep people happy, when you can find this information incredibly easily. I just don't really care to lie in general.

When I say "this is due to Autism", I don't mean "no one experiences this *except* Autistic people". I mean "I experience these things to a degree that they can severely impact my day-to-day quality of life, *because* of Autism." Nor do I mean all autistic people experience this, or that it's *solely* Autism. Parts of it are also trauma and anxiety. Also, Autism is not a monolith, we each have different experiences, even if we have a lot of shared ones.

I also don't mean that this could never be anything else. Maybe I'll find out I was wrong, though I would be surprised. As of right now, this fits my life experiences and the things I deal with every day the best out of all other possible ideas and theories. Could I find a better theory? Sure. Just like physicists may find that the Standard Model might not be correct, right now, it's what we have that fits the best.

Anyways, emotions.

My face doesn't always show how I feel, it's often disconnected from it. I can fake it, but then it looks over the top. I've gotten better, but that masking takes energy from me. Yes, I am happy if I say so, even if what I'm saying sounds flat, or if I look upset. Other times I'm not happy when I look like that, and I have spent my life saying I'm happy to people please.

Do you see the problem involved here with healing?

"So it's trauma and people pleasing, not Autism?"

Yes, and also no. I feel like it's a mix of both. Emotions, when you have Autism, can be a lot. You can have meltdowns. You cry, scream, ramble, curl up, and often, parents take it as "misbehaving", so you are punished. Eventually, this teaches you to mask, and removes you from fully understanding your emotions. It's a mixture of Autism and trauma.

Sometimes Autism causes you to have these giant seemingly out of proportion responses to stimuli. When you are Autistic, these things feel incredibly overwhelming and sometimes painful, so that's why the response is so great. Other times you're disconnected from them, you dissociate or shutdown. This can be due to Autism causing that, or trauma telling you to "never mind that warning sign there, best to never look into it", and you dissociate.

Of course, a society that tells people to downplay emotions doesn't help.

Eventually, you start to unpack it all, and it takes you a long time to learn everything. You have to train yourself to listen to your body and reconnect to your emotions.

They're still big. Sometimes you have these powerful emotional responses to things, and you have to ride the tidal wave. Sometimes you have no reaction. Sometimes your reaction happens minutes, hours, days, weeks, months, years, or decades later. Sometimes you can't identify what the emotion is. Is this anger or overstimulation? Is this envy or a desire to do more for me in my life? Is this sadness or did I forget to eat? Is this guilt or am I overly tired or hungover? Is this jealousy or abandonment trauma? Is this fear, or do I understand the severity of the situation or is it intuition? Am I actually happy to help someone do something, or am I just doing what I think I have to in order to keep people around?

I understand that this is something almost anyone can feel, but for me, this is constant. Almost every emotion, almost every time. A deluge of overthinking, constantly, without end. Every action. Every word. Every thought. Every emotion. Every sensation. Everything. This is why meltdowns and shutdowns happen, it is so easy for your brain to become completely overloaded.

I'm learning to reconnect with my emotions and body. I know I will still have Autism. I will have meltdowns. I will still have difficulty with emotions and that is ok. I'm glad to at least be reconnecting and working with them when I can, enough to improve my life.

At the same time, as much as I know where it comes from, I still don't view Autism as something I hate. Like anything, there are parts I like, and parts I don't like. It also doesn't mean I can act however I want, either. I have to still work on myself. I just know that I need to not hate myself for these things, while I work on them. I wouldn't trade my brain and how it works for anything most days. It can be so difficult and yet so beautiful too.

I just want to learn how to understand myself and how to know what my needs are.

Then it's over for you hoes.

Self-worth

I really thought that I was not good enough because of what others said about me, and how they treated me. I spent decades doing that. I decided I wasn't good enough for anything because of their opinions. I listened to their counsel over defining my own worth. I heeded their words, and internalized that people not liking me, not being attracted to me, not liking my ideas, not talking to me, being too busy, whatever, meant I was somehow "bad".

I feel so dumb but not in a self-hating way, like "oh my goodness, *of course*," kind of way. I know, now, it was due to trauma, abuse, and neglect in various ways that led me down that path. Now, I can look back and know I always had worth. I can see that these were either misunderstandings, people who didn't value me or themselves, or genuinely were assholes. I understand that none of that, NONE OF THAT, meant I was unworthy of love, respect, kindness, compassion, empathy, etc.

I feel relieved. I was holding onto this judgment my whole life. I don't have to be condemned to a life of self-hatred, loneliness, pain, or negativity. I know people will hate me. People will leave. But at least now I know it's not because I'm unworthy. I might fuck up and need to learn and need to heal and need to be better, but I am not inherently unworthy.

I spent so long in a real hell. Not some biblical one, but rather one of personal shame, guilt, hatred, and isolation.

All of that to realize I could walk away free by changing my perspective. Do I always remember this? No. Some days I am still deep in those old feelings. That's how it goes. Sometimes things take a bit longer to learn and heal.

Chasing my own peace

I feel so weary
Constantly trying to find love in others
Even the people who are supposed to love me
And yes, I know they do, and yet I was so often

alone
unheard
criticized
talked over

Why now, as I finally am gaining a sense of self-love
Appreciation for who I am, a sense of peace
Why do I throw that away
Just to chase another person's affection?

Maybe I am being unfair
I can't tell anymore
I feel like it's not so much anyone else
And just echos of former pain
Drowning out all other thoughts and feelings

I want to feel like I mean something to someone
I know I do, I know I do
But sometimes when you look at your phone
And the only notifications you have for days
Are the pings of brands wanting your money
You feel so insignificant

I'm trying to break these stories in my head
That I mean nothing to anyone
Or that I will always be optional
Replace them with honoring myself
My needs
My emotions
My boundaries

Reminding myself that I am loved
Worthy of love
Surrounded by love

I don't need to chase
No one needs to chase me
Why do some talk about chasing
In all of these discussions of love
As though it were some comforting metaphor

Can I not just be me
Wholly me

Then when someone is interested in me
And they show me in beautiful ways
They tell me in wonderful words
How they feel about me
I will finally be secure and open
To show them how I feel

Loving Myself

Am I the drama?

One of the biggest issues I have with self-esteem is when someone's behavior changes, I immediately think it's my fault. I've clearly upset them. I said something that was weird. I pushed them away, or worse, hurt them in some way.

The thing is, that's not generally true. Yes, I should make sure I'm not being harmful. However, to assume I always am, tells me that I don't value myself. Sometimes, there are other things going on, and it's not always about me. That sounds easy to think of, right? Unfortunately, when you've had people blame you for a lot of their issues, through some kind of emotional abuse, you eventually believe it. When someone is consistently highly critical of you and your actions, you tend to think that what you do is an issue.

Of course, constantly blaming yourself for the changes in others isn't very helpful. It causes you to be overly apologetic, insecure, and feel like a burden on others. All of which can harm your various relationships.

I'm trying to shift that narrative in my head. One way is through sitting with the emotions. "Yes, maybe I have hurt them" and I just feel that feeling until it passes. It is a form of meditation, one that reminds us that we're not our thoughts, our emotions, or our stories. You distance yourself from judgment and instead allow yourself to sit in truth. Even if the feeling is uncomfortable. Once I am less attached to that story, I can look at everything and learn how to be better, how to be kinder, and how to make things right, if needed.

Another is to remind myself that they have a lot of other things going on too. Sure, if I said something and suddenly they're quiet, I can probably realize that there's something to work through. People have a lot going on, and I'm most likely not the cause of what's up. I challenge the assumptions I have through "this is just a story that I'm telling myself, I don't know for certain."

After a while, that chatter in your mind shifts from "they're mad at me" to "they're quieter, I don't know why." Instead of forcing a narrative, I allow the situation to be what it is. Their behavior has changed. I don't know why.

Then, without feeling like I'm in trouble, I can reach out, and ask them how they're doing. If they're mad at me, hopefully, they would tell me, and we can work through it. If they can't, then I can't do anything about it, right? If they need support, then I can help out.

The problem is assuming the other shoe will drop. It most likely will not.

Lessons from my jealousy

I like being cherished and having security. Whenever I didn't feel this security, I would feel jealous and think I had to do something about it. I didn't spend time processing it at all, though. Instead of noting the insecurity, checking on my needs and boundaries and how everything fits in, I would get triggered and react, afraid of being hurt. I don't want to be that person anymore. I don't want to just react immediately based on emotions. I want to honor them, and learn how to communicate my needs instead of acting purely on reaction.

While I have said that I want to be claimed, to be cherished, to feel secure, I need my own independence too. At the same time, I want anyone I'm ever partnered with to have the same. I don't think that has to be mutually exclusive. I think you can have something that feels deeply secure while being independent. People do this all the time, right?

I can also be my own source of security, and be present in how things exist here and now.

Jealousy as a feeling isn't bad until I use that feeling in a way that seeks control. On its own, it is just saying "Hey, we feel insecure about this right now. We should figure this out and maybe do something about it" rather than "WE NEED TO TAKE IMMEDIATE ACTION FROM A PLACE OF TERROR!!!!"

The lesson is I need to be in the present and not worry about a future that doesn't even exist. I need to be secure in myself and my ability to always find my own center even after the Tower falls. I need to find ways to manage my stress around change and uncertainty. I need to reflect on my needs and boundaries. I need to understand them. Then I can see if this jealousy is somehow telling me that these are being unmet. I need to also know that I'm worthy as I am and I don't have to worry about it.

I know there are more lessons from throughout the decades but these are some of the bigger ones I remember. I spent decades not listening and like anything in our shadow and emotions unheard and unseen, it will just get more boisterous. The funny thing is, in holding space for my jealousy, I feel more secure in myself than I ever have. I feel I myself am more heard and seen.

So many of these things are interrelated. Neglect and abandonment trauma bleed into fears I have about relationships of any kind. They turn into issues with trust and self-worth. They cause you to seek out escapist ideas of love and romance, and establish a lens of jealousy instead of security.

It's not even two sides of one coin, it's like many faces on a die instead.

Now I'm seeking out myself. I'm not really seeking out a relationship for the first time in a long time because I realize I need me time. This isn't to say I will never date anyone ever again. I'm just making myself a priority. I'm letting go of fear for the first time in a long time.

I still need to socialize, because I still feel lonely and that's ok. That's a feeling too, one I can listen to, and one I can honor. I can reach out to the people I love when I feel that way. At the same time, I'm not trying to just fix that by saying a relationship will solve all my problems because it won't.

I know that now. Weirdly, jealousy, my fear, told me I needed to look at my security more than anything else—I just needed to listen.

You are not your bad thoughts

You are not your bad thoughts. You can let them go. You can challenge them, say "that's not who I am, that's not what I believe, that's not who I am anymore, etc."

A lot of people, if not maybe everyone, have thoughts they wish they didn't have. Anger, hatred, malice, self-loathing; it doesn't matter, they're all just thoughts. Weird biochemical things bubble up. Just like any other thought.

You can be aware of them and let them go.

The trauma dilemma

Am I taking time to become secure and love myself? Or am I just being hyper-independent again and hiding because I don't dare have needs and emotions? "It's ok, I don't need anything, I'm good. No, I don't have emotions, it's ok! Do you need anything?"

Fuck everyone who has ever belittled others for their needs and emotions. Fuck everyone that taught them that the people you trust hurt you.

I'm taking this time and I'm healing ancient wounds from my childhood onward. I know it's good that I am. I just wish I didn't have to.

Love as an autistic woman

I feel like I'm learning how to love with Autism, and I don't blame my condition. I love how my brain works. Well, most of the time. It's both incredible and challenging. What I don't love, is that so much out there is geared toward neurotypical people. If it is "for Autistic people", it's written by a neurotypical person who is going off of rigid stereotypes and ideas of how our brains work. "Representation matters" but we're going to have people outside of the marginalized group who don't understand the nuance and complexity create everything.

When you feel things so deeply in emotions and senses, and have this rich inner world, it can be a lot. You often need to isolate yourself to relax. Just as often, you need to spend time sifting through your emotions and senses to figure out an issue. If you do not, you risk a loud and intense public meltdown, and then people will judge or punish you for it. Even so, I still love how my brain works. I don't see it as this terrible thing, I see that the world doesn't allow us to be us, to work with who we are.

I was forced through the consequences of shutting myself down for others. I learned to mask. I have to isolate myself to accommodate people who won't do the same for me. I have to downplay emotions and interests. It's exhausting.

I understand people have their own needs and boundaries too. As such, I advocate for mine, and I understand when people say that it's too much and walk away. Is it? Not for everyone, but it was for them, and that hurts, and that's ok.

And I know I'm not the only one. I see people like me on social media talking about how difficult it is to exist in this world as Autistic people. We all share similar pains and issues, and connecting with each other helps. It helps to see that I'm not the only one.

So here I am, learning to be by myself but also in groups. I am learning how to unmask. I am learning to advocate for my needs and boundaries while also not burning myself out. I am learning to not hate myself for what happens when I do burn out, shutdown, or meltdown. I am learning to not hate myself for having needs. I am learning to not hate myself for being Autistic.

I spent years hating myself for many reasons. I hated myself for not understanding my emotions, my mind, and my communication. I finally understand. I can look at myself and think, "holy shit, how did I not see you until now?"

I didn't see me.

I didn't hear me.

I didn't love me.

Weirdly all of my bumblings, mishaps, pain, frustration, toxicity, healing, atonement, research, and crying due to love and loss, all of it led me to myself. Now I just need to keep seeing me, keep hearing me, keep advocating for me, keep learning about me, keep unlearning toxicity for me, keep improving for me, keep loving me, and realize I am always worthy of love, as I am.

I love myself, as I am. The healing isn't to remove or

hide my Autism. It is not to make myself palatable. My healing is to love it, and myself, and I finally do.

The Fool

At a certain point, you can stay where you feel uninspired, stagnant, unloved, and unsupported, but comfortable because it's easy to stay still. Or you can take a leap into the unknown. It may be scary, but something keeps tugging at you from within your subconscious.
Don't you feel it?
That yearning to be free, yearning to be loved, yearning to be supported, yearning to be understood, yearning to be creative.
I hope you take that leap.

What the fuck are boundaries?

So I've talked a lot about boundaries in this book, but seriously, what the fuck are they? To put it simply, they are us communicating how we protect our autonomy and self. Boundaries set an expectation as to how you wish to be treated. Boundaries typically happen before limits, but not always, as sometimes the boundaries have been pushed for decades and the limit is here.

That's a lot to say, but what does it all mean? Boundaries start with saying "no" to things. No can be a complete sentence, but you can also offer additional information if you want. "No, I will not help you with that report, I am already working on my own PowerPoint for some meeting." Yes, you can set boundaries at work.

Boundaries also have to do with how you wish to be treated. "My name is Caelynn, anything else is not my name." "I am a woman, I do not care how you think or feel about the matter, as it is my own sense of self, and that is not negotiable." These are closer to limits, but either way, boundaries are an invitation to the other person to treat you properly.

What other boundaries can you set? I've set boundaries with my parents in the past where I could not pay bills for them anymore, as I didn't have the money to do so. I've told my mom that I cannot come over on a Sunday to spend time with them, as I need to have my own time to rest after a lot of events. I've told people not to touch me without permission. I've told people who were making fun of me to stop. Boundaries are protection, they're you sticking up for yourself.

Boundaries can be difficult to determine. When you've been a people pleaser for a long time, you have a hard time finding out what you do want to do, and what you don't. The thoughts are there, but the drive to follow through with a "No" is not there. We've all wanted to say "No" to events, tasks, whatever, and then still say "Sure". Boundaries take practice and encouragement, and sometimes there is conflict.

When people expect you to say some kind of "Yes" all of the time, they do not like it when you finally say, "No". People do not like losing unfettered access to someone's time, energy, labor, and other resources. That's not your fault, and you still deserve to have your boundaries respected. How you handle this is up to you. You can explain why you said "No", but that might mean to them that they need to argue with you to get you to say "Yes". If that sounds manipulative, that's because it is. People should be able to handle rejection without you having to take care of them.

Other times, if you explain the boundary, they will understand more context and what exactly is the issue. Maybe they don't want unfettered access, they just want to understand your boundaries better. This can help them avoid future oversteps. Usually, this looks more like, "Thank you for setting a boundary. Is there anything else I should be aware of?" Or "I understand. Can I have a bit more context, so that I understand how to communicate more respectfully?" There is an acknowledgment and acceptance of the boundary, and then a request for more information, and this is important–specifically to avoid more issues. They're not trying to challenge the boundary. Sometimes they might apologize too, depending.

Speaking of apologies, you do not need to apologize for setting a boundary. At all. This is your autonomy, you do not owe them anything more than mutual respect and honesty, right? You are not doing anything wrong by setting any boundaries.

Boundaries are also changeable, and that's ok. If someone challenges you on that, it is up to you if you want to explain why. The thing is, we're changing creatures. What was painful a few years ago, might not be now. What we allowed before, might be too much for us now. Maybe we allow some people to do certain things, but not others. These are valid reasons, and you don't have to explain it to them, unless you want to.

Boundaries are not a way to seek control. You cannot use them to tell someone how to live *their* life. You cannot set a boundary saying they cannot enjoy their hobbies because they have to spend more time with you. That is a want or a need, and you can communicate that. "I would like to spend more time with you. Can we have a few nights a week where it's just us?" That is open and communicative. It allows a conversation that builds up the relationship, where everyone has their autonomy respected. Boundaries are a conversation, not an ultimatum.

That ultimatum part is an important distinction. Boundaries are a conversation of respect, not a tactic to get someone to do what you want. Ultimatums come with a desire to control someone else. "Do this or else". That is coercion. Boundaries say, "This is how I want to be treated. If you cannot, then it might be time to figure out where we go from here." The key difference is you're not doing this to control someone, you're doing this to respect and protect yourself. Some people may try to say they're the same, or that boundaries that result in breakups are also coercive, but they're not. The difference is control–if you try to make them do something they don't want to do, that's coercion. If you ask them to respect you, and they do not, and you decide you should go for your safety and health, that's protection. Be wary of people who conflate the two, or say you're being unfair, unkind, or manipulative. Why would they think that your asking for respect is manipulation? That sounds like they are projecting their own issues.

Lastly, boundaries are a conversation. They're meant to make a relationship stronger, not give one power over the other. Their entire point is to stand up against power dynamics and unhealthy behaviors. They root out abuse and manipulative behavior, pulled like weeds from a garden, to show you what's beneath. If you set a boundary and people accept it? That's a green flag. Are they upset and trying to stop it? Red flag.

This is what I have learned in my own life. It is not a perfect system, as nothing is. This is the basis that I start with in my own relationships. When I find issues or learn something new, I revise it. I suggest working with mental health professionals, and researching further. It is a skill

Loving Myself

that requires practice.
   I hope you protect yourself.

7

Love

Love, like anything else, is a skill. Not something just for romance and fairy tales, but something we do for ourselves, our loved ones, and our community. It requires effort and practice.

You might not like this one

Welcome to the last chapter of my book. Now we're going to talk about real, non-toxic love. You might not like this chapter on love, because it's honest. Love isn't often enemies to friends or lovers. It's not a RomCom where the guy is "persistent" [derogatory]. It's not that person who has not committed, being your "twin flame in separation". They likely don't feel the same way you do.

I know that sounds harsh, but I have a question for you. Would you rather wait for someone who is not interested at this time and most likely will not be later, or realize that they don't feel that way and walk away? With the latter, you get to find someone who is interested in you. Doesn't that sound better?

Reluctantly, I'm beginning to consider myself a love witch* [amongst many other workings]. I have watched so many RomComs. I have read quite a few romance novels and comics. I have gone through it with love and rejection and abandonment. All of this, to learn enough to break my own cycles, and maybe help others end them too. This helps them be who they're meant to be, and draw in who they're meant to be, *if* they're meant to.

Not everyone has to have a lifelong relationship, and that's okay. We should all be able to have or not have what we want in our lives. We should not have to live up to societal expectations.

Further, a lot of these narratives around love are those same patriarchal societal expectations. The masculine is tortured. The feminine heals him. He's persistent, but really it's more predatory and painful to watch. Though I still do, RomComs are my junk food, though I am finding that I just can't watch some of them anymore. It's just too junky. In the end, it sets up this narrative of how things should go.

This narrative that everything must be difficult, and everyone has strict gender roles in romance. The masculine must do the work to win her over when she hates him at first. They have to have a toxic relationship that their friends hate, but **"damn our friends, they don't know us!"** They have to fumble through, he needs to realize that the girl he met at a bar isn't *her* before he rushes back to her, love renewed. And don't even get me started that most mainstream romantic movies are cisgender, heterosexual, and white. Anyone else is pushed to the side as comedic relief–we're just there to be interesting filler for the story.

And so on, and so forth. This could be its own book.

Not every romance or RomCom has these ideas. Many of these themes are done to add drama and suspense to the movie. Even so, the majority of these movies follow a similar path. The thing is, we don't have to do it like this. There are some really good, non-toxic romantic stories out there that still have drama and suspense!

Yet here we are, the romance market flooded with toxicity. This sets the standard for a lot of people and their relationships. There is a lack of good representation. There is often a lack of healthy relationships in these stories too.

People think that love in real life requires suspense,

drama, and unnecessary conflict. Even though it will already have enough of all of that as is, without adding more. Love is messy and difficult at times, don't get me wrong. I just think we add so much challenge on top of it with expectations, loyalty tests, and projection, all from our favorite RomComs and romance stories.

Maybe that's my own projection. I only have my own viewpoint. I have had my own difficulties with love. I have dealt with abandonment and neglect, and when I have tarot readings that tell me someone is coming back, I am tempted to put my hope into that. I have held onto the hope that one day, the person I like will like me, because that's how the story goes, right? I have to believe.

So now we're going to spend a chapter on that. Now it's time to talk about what love really should be, and should not be.

Why am I reluctant to call myself a love witch? It conjures up this idea of someone using magic to force someone into love, and I don't like that. To me, this is more a type of working that helps people love themselves, see what keeps them from non-toxic love, and how to work on that. I know there is love magic that is safe for all involved, and there are many schools of thought on whether love magic respects or ignores free will—that's its own thesis, and we don't need to go into it, because I don't do love magic other than self-love magic, healing magic, drawing in the correct person, and maybe one day I will do hand-fasting ceremonies for people who want to commit to one another. As such, I haven't spent much time on it, nor do I want to speculate on it, because I don't know love workings between people, I know self-love workings, and have been doing them for a few years now. Plus, I am most likely wrong about love workings, so I just leave it alone.

Either way, this is not The Love Witch, which, is a great movie, and an excellent example of how NOT to love.

Atonement

Hekate told me once that "some people come here to learn difficult lessons"*. She would know, she certainly has led me through far too many crossroads in this lifetime alone. That's not even getting into any other lifetimes, or the countless others she has guided. Each crossroad, is another chance to learn lessons. Painful lessons at times. Learning to be kind or continuing to be cruel or whatever you want to call it in each situation.

Some people can't let go of that. They stay cruel. They don't reflect on how to get out of that situation or how to get out of that toxic mindset. They don't care that they are harmful. Of course, there is always nuance. Always.

Instead, we can listen to that feeling, pulling us from being harmful. We can hold space for all the pain and shadow and regret. We can learn to love ourselves and others. Further, we might need to heal, by going through the pain of realizing that we're harming others. We might have grown up never wanting to harm anyone. We sometimes still do because we lose sight of ourselves, and what we value.

This isn't about shaming anyone. This isn't about sin and hell, using fear to chastise like some might. No. That keeps us locked in fear and shame, without learning our lessons. This is about reminding us that we don't have to keep our heads low in shame about things we regret. Learn the lessons, make amends if needed, and be better.

We can let all of that go and heal now. We can heal our

inner child by remembering who we were when we were younger before people projected their issues and insecurities and systems onto us and we were our unique selves. We can do that so that we do not carry those same issues with us, breaking that cycle. We may still hurt people and lose them. We may have to atone in whatever ways are necessary. But we can change and learn our lessons in this life so that we can carry that knowledge with our souls into the next one. Or, at the very least, live better in this life, if there are no other lives.

This is not meant to be spiritual bypassing or fatalistic or deterministic or an explanation of why shitty things are shitty. Sometimes shit is shit and that's it. It's more an acknowledgment of the work put in to be better after making mistakes. It's a work of unlearning, understanding the difficult things that happen because of my own foolishness, and the lessons I learned along the way. Not every bad thing in my life was a lesson—some were just shitty fucking trauma and it hurt. It hurt. Yet other things were lessons. At least, this is how I understand it, and how Hekate and I have spoken of things. Some things just suck, some things are awesome, some things are lessons, and some things are gifts.

The end of time

Meet me at the end of time
Where all things cease to be
And you can walk along with me
Forever, truly free

Meet me in that silent void
Where nothing can make sound
Yet still we sing and laugh out loud
In unending cacophony

Meet me in the liminal
Where moonlight glows around
A place we both can dance and bound
Across an endless moonlit sea

Love

Imagine how wonderfully kind you will be

Imagine how wonderfully kind you will be
When you are surrounded by loving people
All the gifts you will give, and the space you will hold
For people who offer the same.

Instead of remembering the shame you have felt
For being let down and letting down
You can heal in this moment, right here and now
By celebrating the ways you have grown.

Feel the trauma, lifting away, as you see your real face
No longer masking, surviving, surrounded by lies
An end to the voices, twisting your mind,
Telling you that you are cruel, when really, you've always been kind.

You are everything

Being around you has been so

Healing

It's nothing specific
Not an exact word
Or series of actions
Just who you are
Everything about you
Speaks to my mind
My heart
My soul.

I expect nothing of you
Not in some cruel way

You are everything

It's more that I don't want to use you for healing
Nor expect you to be something you are not
I want to accept you
Wholly
As you are
Each and every moment

And yet the healing just happens

You are wonderful

Love

I am immeasurably grateful
To have met you again in this lifetime

New phones

I want to save every conversation
Savor your words again and again
Until my phone runs out of space
And I need a new one
Do you feel the same?
Maybe we could get new phones

Together

Let the hours melt away
As we spend precious moments
Adding it all to my journals
Photos of us taking up more space
As we leave to go on our own
I save everything I can

Damn

My phone is out of space again
Is yours too?
Maybe we could get new phones

Together

Confidence!

If you like someone and they're available, but you don't let them know, how will anything ever begin? Or, if you've been flirting, and you like them, but you never say it, don't be shocked if they walk away! A question that is not asked, is always answered by a no. I'll say again, if you like someone, *tell* them.

"But what if they don't like me?" Then you're still where you are now, but at least you know for sure and can move on. I understand. I wouldn't tell people that I liked them, because I was dealing with my own wounds around abandonment and reject. I completely understand if you are too. You may need to journal about it, feel through it, and release it.

At the same time, I've been rejected *a lot*. That's not me bragging about my impressive ability to get the no, it's to let you know that the more you put yourself out there and are rejected, the less it hurts. There will still be instances where it does, but *usually* that's because I've built it all up in my mind and heart. I've built this idea of how things *should* go, and when they don't, I feel hurt. And also, I still have rejection sensitive dysphoria, and rejection in general can hurt. That's ok.

But it will hurt worse if you keep building it up in your mind, rather than asking and finding out. I did that, and that hurt was my own fault, because I let it drag on and become something more than it was in my own heart. Don't let it go too long and build up. Let them know how you feel. Maybe it will go well, maybe it won't, but I can assure you, you will be ok in the end. It definitely will be better after a good cry.

One last thing, don't be weird about it. This isn't to shame, I'm saying, I have been weird, I have been stupid, I have been creepy, I have been awkward in how I put myself out there. So I'm not coming from a place of judgment, but of guidance. Take the time to calm down, breathe, maybe rehearse something out in your head that is meaningful and honest, be level headed, you know? At the same time, be yourself. You don't need antics. You don't need tricks. If someone doesn't like you, they're not right for you. Like I said elsewhere with rejection, that doesn't mean anything bad on them. We all feel differently about people. Someone else will like you for you.

At the same time, if you fuck up like I have, you learn. You become better at communicating. I just hope you can learn through me here and put your best self forward.

Also note for the men who read this who are too close to falling into an incel pipeline—don't listen to pickup artists, and don't listen to misogynist podcasts. For fuck's sake, have some women friends who are ONLY friends and talk to them about life. The way these toxic men view things, and tell you how to view things, are based on an echo chamber.

Grow out of the toxic bubble you have been in. Have friends that are not cisgender, heterosexual, men, or white. Talk with socialists and communists. Learn from other religions and the people who practice them. Go to a therapist. Learn some empathy. And *listen*, don't try to be a "debate bro".

You might learn a new wonderful thing in life. You might become a better version of yourself. You might find real confidence and love yourself. You might even find a healthy relationship through being a decent person with an awesome personality who doesn't blame all of your *own* problems on others. Also stop asking women at the gym to take out our headphones, stop saying we look better without makeup, stop telling us to smile, stop catcalling us, stop following us, stop that shit. That's not "shooting your shot", that's creepy.

While everyone deserves love, no one has to put up with our toxic bullshit, right? Right. It wouldn't be fair for someone else to have to go through hell for us to feel loved. Also, remember there are so many ways to have love in your life, from yourself, your community, without having to make someone into your manic pixie dream girl or some bullshit like that.

As for the rest of you, who aren't compensating your own issues with shitty ideas, go out into the world with confidence, and flirt respectfully and safely.

When we go to Paris

I like to listen to Parisian cafe jazz playlists
Smooth yet lilting
Imagining a Brie and butter sandwich
On a toasty, warm baguette
Sharing a morning moment at a corner cafe
With the love of my life
Quietly
Before walking through the old, romantic architecture
The narrow side streets and houses
Hundreds of years old
Back before the world shut down
Holding hands, smiling, drinking all of the beauty in
Winding our way from the apartment
With a cute view we rented for the week
Finding ourselves in an hours long line,
Hoping just to catch a glimpse
Of the smirking Mona Lisa that I swore never smiled
Maybe that was a different universe
A past life somewhere else
Laughing, discussing the universe and existence
Just how bizarre it all is
Eating croissants with the preserves we brought
For the moment we became peckish
A life easy and beautiful
It still could be...someday
Will I know when we meet
Who you are to me?

Love

Maybe it will be clear
When we go to Paris
Should the world start up again.

Can we not run away

Can we not run away, you and I?
Some place far from here?
Where people don't ask us
Endless questions of who we are
And shoot us dirty looks
Maybe the drive isn't so far
Can we not move far away
Maybe to some coastal town
Somewhere with rain and mist
Ocean smells and cooling breezes
Or somewhere warm and sunny?
Where the nights are long
And full of laughter and music
Magic and wonder
Can we not move far away
You and I
Together
Just this once

A universe of us

I could share worlds with you
Stars unending
Brightly colored nebulae
And the black holes that rip through time
Even if but a moment
We could create a galaxy
To rival the beauty of Andromeda
And the Milky Way themselves
A universe of us
To remember each other by

Judgment

I feel bad for people who judge others. Sure, maybe that's a judgment. It's probably another form of the paradox of tolerance. Even so, I don't understand spending time worrying about what someone else wears, how they look, what job they have, or who they love. I don't understand trying to convince yourself that they're wrong or sinful or whatever.

They're not wrong unless they're harming others or removing their autonomy.

If you're reading this as a Christian, stop applying your rules to everyone else. What was it, remove the plank in your own eye, before trying to remove the speck of sawdust in another's? This isn't even a speck of sawdust, it is love, not sin. A mistranslation at best, and a purposeful witch hunt at worst. Either way, unnecessary and wicked.

I guess that's the heart of this.

Worry about yourself. Support others in the way that they ask. Don't give unneeded and egotistical advice. If someone wants your opinion or advice, they will ask. If someone is harming someone, actively, NOW you can step in.

Also, not liking something is not the same as harm. Someone supporting their LGBTQ children, or teaching factual history about racism, is not harmful, even if it hurts our egos to learn it.

In general, it's best to let people live their own lives as they see fit if they're not harming someone. Otherwise, *you* are the one harming them. ***You*** are removing their autonomy.

This makes *you* the aggressive one, the oppressive one, etc. That's not how anyone should be.

It happened, it hurt me, it wasn't ok, it wasn't my fault, and I'm safe now

Looking back at these moments in the last few years when I began healing trauma, it's clear that I was stumbling through it. I have somehow managed to heal a lot of pain, anger, sorrow, and trauma that I held onto for decades. I think a lot of that successful healing was twofold. One, my therapists in 2019-2021 laid a lot of groundwork for a compassionate understanding of my past, myself, emotions, body, and trauma. Two, I was constantly researching and learning about healing work, both psychologically, and spiritually.

What I've learned sounds simple, but the work is difficult and painful. It is not so simple to heal trauma, as you live through those moments again while healing. At the same time, as much as I have healed, I still have moments where I have to recenter. I still have to remind myself that I am loved, lovable, loving, and worthy of love. I still have to challenge old pains and traumas.

I had to recognize what was traumatic and be honest about it. This happened, this hurt, this was not ok, this was not my fault. It was extremely difficult, and requires a lot of compassion and reassurance, which took me time to learn. When I started, I was still very harsh with myself. It took a lot of effort to be kind. In time, it became easier to say kind things. "No, you're not broken. You're not crazy. You're not weird. You've been hurt, and you're healing". The reactions you have had when triggered by memories or flashbacks are not something that is bad. This is something that is normal and happens due to trauma responses.

If you're in that phase of healing, be kind to yourself. Please, don't feel too bad that it takes time sometimes to learn how to even *be* kind to ourselves. We're doing the best we can, with what we have, each and every day.

When looking at my own trauma, I had to remember how rejection felt. I had to remember how loneliness felt. I had to remember how abandonment felt. In some cases, I had to remember how it felt in that moment when it was a present sensation. I had to feel it in my body, where does it hurt, where is it stored? What emotions and memories come up? How can I be here for myself now, in ways where I didn't have the support then?

I had to feel those difficult emotions, and allow them to just be. I had to give myself permission to just be sad, without immediately trying to fix it. I had to allow myself to not pretend that I was ok. I had to remind myself that I was not bad for healing and not being productive. Some days, and some *weeks,* it was a struggle just to keep me fed and clean. Cleaning my apartment was a challenge. Often, I couldn't do any of it. I just couldn't*.

Thoughts would pop up like "I will always be alone. I'm disgusting. I'm unlovable. People hate me. Etc." I had to separate these thoughts from the original event. I came to understand that the original event held so much pain. Pain that was difficult to feel and also continue functioning, so my ego stepped in. These thoughts were ego-based ways to protect me that was a *reaction* to that event, not part of the event itself. It may not sound like it but think of it as more a negative protection. I know the stove is hot by remembering the pain, so I do not touch the stove. These thoughts were like that, but they were focusing on me and blaming myself. I needed to change that.

I had to hold space for that pain, and also challenge those thoughts with compassion. This allowed me to let go of the guilt and shame that I built up through the trauma. "I have not always been alone, nor will I be. I'm not disgusting, even if someone thinks that or says that I know I am beautiful. People leave for their own reasons, things end because everything has a season, but that does not mean I am unlovable. Some people might hate me, but that does not mean everyone will. Some people hate me because of their own insecurities and that is not my fault. Some people hate me because you can't make everyone happy. Some people hate me because they don't like that I hold boundaries now and respect myself and my needs. Etc."

There is a need to feel safe too. It's difficult to do that while facing past trauma, but there are many ways to go about that. Getting back into your body through sensation and movement. Spending time observing your emotions and thoughts. Taking on different roles to see from new viewpoints. Expressing yourself through creativity. **Resting**. Showing compassion towards yourself. There are so many ways to do it.

Sometimes I would try to hold compassion for myself, and it wouldn't work. So, I had to work through it in many ways. I would dance, write poetry, and breathe through it, while feeling and remembering what happened. I had conversations with my ancestors and deities to gain new perspectives. I got high. I cried and ate wonderfully indulgent foods, releasing emotions and also activating that dopamine. I would orgasm.

Pleasure and sex, and consequently, sex magic, are powerful healers. They can take you to another state of consciousness where you can really get into reprogramming how you feel about your body, your thoughts, and your security. You can speak intentions in that time after to help your mind solidify that thinking into being within you.

All of these are ways you can get into your body. All of these are ways you can work to rest, recover, and recuperate. There unfortunately isn't a cure-all. Every trauma heals in different ways for every different person, and we have so many ways to work through it. As you show up for yourself, again, and again, and again, it does get easier over time, as you heal.

I recommend that you work with a trauma-informed professional too. This work can be incredibly difficult. You may have shame centered on your body, pleasure, productivity, rest, and more. You may accidentally harm yourself more by re-experiencing those memories. Make sure that you have a safe environment to heal within, and if you do not, try to find a community that can help you get out of an unsafe environment.

If you have a friend who has told you they're struggling, if they're up for it, cook or clean for them, or pick something up from the store for them. This is how we help build community and start helping each other when capitalism is just too fucking much. We're already told to be individualistic, don't be too much, don't be a burden—and we wonder why so many people harm themselves. How can people come to us for help when we all shy away or act like helping each other is some burden? Yes, we need boundaries. We also need community. Finding a healthy balance between those two is essentially for us to survive and thrive.

Love and detachment

I feel like much of my life has been a large lesson in love and detachment. That I can love, and love unconditionally, and not want to possess, control, obsess, worry, cling. I experienced so much insecurity in love, relationships, family, and friendships, that I carried with me every time after. These experiences forced me to sit down, and learn to detach from any expectations or hopes in a non-existent future.

I still have days where I feel those attachments. I still feel fear. I still experience loneliness. I still want security. In holding onto these things, there is suffering. I was pierced by two arrows: pain, then suffering.

The first arrow was the pain I felt from an event. The second was my attachment or resistance to the first arrow, causing further suffering. This is further explained by the Buddha in the Sallatha Sutta, or the Parable of Two Arrows, found within the Samyutta Nikaya.

I had wounds from rejection, abandonment, neglect, and trauma. I then worried that these wounds meant I would always be alone, hurt, unlovable, and unworthy. I feared people leaving, rejection, and loss. These wounds caused me to fear that everyone would leave eventually. That was my second arrow. I became attached to people, resisting any change due to worry and fear of loss, because of this second arrow, this suffering.

I have spent so much of my time, through self-reflection and studying, fumbling my way through

Buddhism and learning how to live without attachment, at this moment. I never really planned to seek out Buddhism, witchcraft, paganism, pantheism, omnism, and animism*. These are things in some cases figured out through reflection and experience. In some other cases, I learned them in deep and vulnerable conversations with excellent people. In still other cases, I found them in research and learning that helped me understand the universe and my place in it, what I want, how to be present, and to let go.

I am not perfect at this, of course. I have entire libraries to learn. I will have fear and worry, and need to work through it again. When I get attached again, or have fear and worry, then it is time to breathe. To sit with it. To feel through it. To know it is not permanent. To be.

I believe that any deity can exist, as another facet of an ever-expressive universe, for better or worse. I believe that thoughts can breathe life into thought forms through focused effort and intent, and this is how many entities and deities are made, while others are just spirits and entities that grew over time. To me, many things have their own spirit, and again, this is another facet of an ever-expressive universe. Buddhism is something that has helped me understand my own place within this universe in many ways and has also helped me have a better understanding of myself, who I am, and my own mind, spirit, and body. As I am a white woman, I also have to make sure that I am respectful in how I learn about Buddhism, and who I support while learning.

I will make mistakes, and when I do, then I will have to learn how to be better, how to be more respectful, and not do it again. This is what accountability is, not perfection, but respect, and choosing respect of others and their boundaries over preservation of some perceived self, every time. Learning new ideas from other cultures is amazing, but if they say something is closed, then stay the fuck out. It is wild to me how people will talk about respecting personal boundaries and consent and then just disregard another culture's boundaries and consent and just steal from them. Like...do you not understand how that is bad?

The storm is passing

Lately, whenever I have difficult wounds come up, I notice that my mental chatter is different. Times when I feel I'm not worthy of love, or that no one could ever love me, do not hold as much sway over me. Yes, the wound still comes up. It still hurts, and I cry. Even so, while I'm crying and releasing, my thoughts are more positive. The wound still hurts. A million negative wounded thoughts swirl. Yet, as I'm feeling through that pain, I have new wonderful thoughts now, that help me through it. "This is only temporary!", "You're doing so well!", "Keep releasing this pain!", "Yes, you've had a lot of difficult things happen, but that doesn't mean it will always be that way!" And so on, and so forth.

I spent decades feeling terrible. The last few years were a particularly nasty storm. In that storm, I finally started allowing myself to heal those wounds. I started paying attention to them, which meant they *hurt worse than they had before*.

At least until now. I've noticed where the pain has shifted in my body. Where once I felt this deep chest pain where my heart is, I am starting to feel it be smaller, less aching, more in like the pit of my stomach.

Finally, I reached this point where I had had enough. "I can't do this anymore. I can't keep feeling like I'm unworthy. I can't keep feeling like I'm incapable of love, or people hate me. I can't keep longing after people who don't want me, and feeling like someday people will wake up and not love me anymore." Not all at once, mind you, but throughout a week or two.

Things felt clearer.

I know healing isn't linear. I will still have those fears sometimes, I will cry, I will hurt–but I think it will be easier.

I don't know what's coming in my life. I don't know if I will be with anyone, and sometimes, I don't even know if what I've wanted is what I truly want. I'm working through that now, and unpacking "what does love look like to me". Maybe I do still want romance in a lifelong partnership. Maybe I don't. Maybe I do, but it isn't in the way society pushes, this marriage centric view of what successful, committed love is. Maybe there isn't a success, like trying to measure it seems like an expectation to me. Maybe I don't need to live up to the same tired shared illusions of what success is. The American Dream. The Protestant Work Ethic. Climbing the Corporate Ladder. Fame and Notoriety. So on and so forth.

While I'm sorting out the details, I finally feel like I'm worthy of it. It takes the pressure off thinking I have to meet someone and it has to work out immediately, while also slowly building. It was very confusing. "This person has to be my soulmate, no this person, no this person, oh no, maybe they're a twin flame". More mental chatter that was just adding to my freaking out about love, intimacy, passion, friendship, commitment, and whatever, right? It was so much pressure. I don't care. I mean, I care about love, I care about liking someone, but not in a way where I neglect myself right now, for a future that might never be.

All the while, I had been feeling like no one could love me, no one could care about me—of course I've been alone and lonely. How do you start anything positive with all of this negativity? I'm not one for toxic positivity. I don't like to ignore real problems. I would much rather see them as they are and work on them. Yet there I was, literally making up problems that didn't need to exist because of old wounds, and freaking out about the future.

Maybe I'll freak out again, who knows? I just hope that at that time, I have a bit more of an internal compass to help me get back out of the storm.

Temperance

Temperance. Patience. That's a well-known meaning for the card, though temperance itself is derived from tempus*, Latin for time.

It's patience, but moreover, a letting go of control in order to allow time to do its thing. Stepping aside so that things can fall into place at the right time. This doesn't mean you wait for things to just happen, you still have to set out and work towards them. Books don't write themselves. Once the book is written, while we might do more work to promote it, we don't constantly check in on when it's going to be bought. We don't stand at a bookstore staring at it, waiting for someone to read it.

I mean, hopefully, you don't. You need to eat, stay hydrated, and rest at some point!

Temperance is my own personality card in the tarot. You can look up how that works, or read Archetypal Tarot. My card being Temperance seems like a cosmic joke to me, as I am anything except patient. Waiting is anathema to me. I hate time, and I feel I'm often stuck outside of it. I see all the pathways it could take, unsure of which way is up or down, or what will be, waiting for it all to coalesce.

The problem is, though, I get so freaked out about how much better things will be once something happens, that I feel anxious. I want things to be finished, to progress, to move. So much so, that I forget I'm not in the future, I'm right here, right now. Temperance is about the present too. It is a reminder that one waits, one observes time passing, because one lives now.

Things move slowly, build slowly, and unfold slowly, all of it taking time to become. Temperance is an understanding that the things worth the effort, take time to come to fruition. It is the card of alchemy because breaking something down, and reforming it, takes time and patience too. Some spellwork may happen instantaneously, but often it works in the background, taking time while we reside in the present.

This has been one of the more difficult lessons to learn for me. I've been alone so long that I've become attached to future states. I'm not in the future though. I'm in Temperance. Right now, I think I understand this, that good things take time to come into our lives, to unfold, to be. That I can exist here and now as I am, worthy of loving myself, and not waiting for the ghosts of some future.

I hope I don't lose sight of that and become anxious again anytime soon.

Temperance also has to do with temper, or moderation and balance; that's why it is also the card of balance. Temper didn't always mean anger, but your current temperament. It means composure or disposition. To temper is to make new or different through time and temperature, again, alchemy. An even temper, a patient working, and the allowance for time to bring about the result of change from the previous card, Death.

But for this, I'm going with time.

Kindness is not being nice

Nice is being polite to not rock the boat. Nice is staying small to make sure you keep the peace. Nice is not setting boundaries because "you're being mean". Nice is not speaking your truth about what happened because you don't want to hurt them even though they didn't think about how hurt you were.

Kindness says fuck all of that, I won't try to hurt others, but I also will not allow them to hurt me, or get away with it.

Love readings could be better

Maybe I am just a skeptic, who's also a sucker. Is that possible? To be both sides of that coin? I have a lot of issues with love readings, yet I find myself often listening to them. I mean, come on, who doesn't want to believe that love is only an incoming message away?

The problem is, these readings require a heavy amount of discernment, which I think a lot of people lose when they're hoping for something specific to happen. That expectation will often set you up for a Tower moment, and the Three of Swords.

If discernment is not there, it can be harmful, and keep you in situations that are not healthy.

I have some questions that I think will help with discernment:

Why do you want a love reading for a situation that could be solved with open and honest communication, or trusting the communication that has already occurred?

Why do you want a love reading for a situation where you're unsure of how they feel or what they want?

Why do you want a love reading for a situation that broke your heart and you want them back?

Why do you want a love reading for a situation that makes you feel less than or unwanted?

Instead, would you not rather heal? Wouldn't you rather do the internal work to leave those situations, and find a real, honest, open, vulnerable, communicative, non-toxic love?

I would rather see readings that help us heal. Why? As you work on yourself within, you change the situations without. As within, so without, right? This internal work causes us to have more confidence and self-worth. We establish better boundaries. We respect and love ourselves and others. We unlearn toxic ideas and behaviors. All of this work positively affects our relationships.

We might still have tough situations, but we have healthier ways to handle them, and healthier ways to heal if they hurt. This is how I think love readings should go. We should help each other find the right partners for us, rather than holding onto hope in hopeless situations.

Fully

One day
I will be loved
Fully
For who I am

I won't have to be small

They will make me feel as though I am enough
Instead of too little or too much.

They will not try to change me
To have someone different
To make me into someone I am not
But will support me while helping me grow
They will hold boundaries and respect mine

The difference in all of this
Is that their words, their actions
Come from respect and love
Not control and fear
I am learning to be this person too–
For myself and others

No one is perfect, I know this
They will mess up, so will I
We will fight and argue
While holding love in our hearts
Enough to find peace with each other

Love

To heal whatever happened

A balance between us
A give and take born in love
Rather than self-service
Not transactions, but reciprocity

I hope I see it for what it is
That I do not pine after others
Who cannot be this for me
That I do not miss love
Because I don't believe it
That I do not push them away
For fear they will hurt me too
That I do not hurt them
By being too afraid

One day
I will be loved
Fully
For who I am

I can't help but trust you

I could tell you anything, driving through the night
Until I'm exhausted and just trying to stay awake
Let's get lost because we took the wrong highway
And share the drama and laughter from our lives
You mean so much to me that it terrifies me
Usually I don't have the best time letting people in
But I trust you. I can't seem to help that.
You are one of my dearest friends,
Closer to me than most
I can't wait to see where life takes you,
Or where it takes me
Every now and again, we can come back and share
The amazing adventures we have had until we're lost
Only to have another adventure begin.

Loud violence

What if we accepted
that words can be violent
The phrases and jokes
We tell each other
Thinking nothing of them
Can traumatize and harm?
Maybe instead of saying
"It is just a joke"
"Lighten up"
"You are so sensitive"
"Freedom of speech"
We instead say
"I didn't mean to hurt you
But I have
And I am sorry.
Now that I know this
I can be better."
It is so simple–
Being kind and respectful
Why do people try so hard
To be abusive to others?

Sponge

Might I soak up the pain in you
As a sponge I could take away
All of your grief and suffering

Only to be rinsed out

So that all the grime
The sadness, the anger
Can flow down the drain
And far away from you
But I know that I cannot
I know that all of us have
This fullness to us
Each emotion creating art
A life lived fully through and through
It just hurts me to see you

Crestfallen

Bearing the weight of the world
Your world and all of the ruins
Of towers crashing around you
You deserve the best of life
Beauty and passion and a world

Unfucked.

Might I soak up the pain in you

Love

As a sponge I could take away
All of your grief and suffering

Unfortunately I cannot.

So I will be what I am
In order to be here for you

Communication is key

I spend a lot of time talking about communication. Being open. Being vulnerable. Being honest. All of this is important and sounds like I know what I'm doing.
I don't.
I have no idea beyond that. I've been learning as I go, remembering how to be myself and not mask. Setting boundaries that are too harsh or aren't strong enough. Being open but maybe with information people don't need to know. Being honest to a fault. I am still learning and wrote this book as much for myself as I did for anyone else.

I have been working on learning Dialectical Behavioral Therapy, which has tools for communication. I think it's a good starting point. However, with anything, I need to learn from multiple sources to get a well-rounded idea. On top of that, I'm learning what I need, alongside my Autism. How do I wish to be treated? What does love look like to me? How do I want to be desired? There are more than five love languages, there are maybe as many as there are people. This idea of sorting ourselves may help for a quick chat, but every relationship is unique. You need longer conversations than just "I like physical touch and gifts".

This feels so necessary, and yet I have so many questions and so much to learn. Maybe I can start by just asking myself how I felt my past relationships and friendships went. What worked well, and what didn't? What felt like it was communicated well, and what felt like it wasn't? What did I like and what didn't I like? Has any of that changed between then and now?

I've been so externally focused, people pleasing for so long. So many people are so bad at communication, refusing to be honest or having difficult conversations. As a result, I don't always know how to effectively express myself. I've had people get mad because I was honest, direct, and communicative, so I learned to play their game. I masked to avoid confrontation, anger, and to keep surface level relationships. I'm done with that.

I would rather have deep, communicative relationships, and lose the rest if I must. I've been so reflective on my past in all of my healing. It has helped me release a lot of pain, and learn a lot about myself. Now, I work to understand how I want to live in the present. I reflect on how I can draw all this gorgeous love in, in the ways that feel right for me, and be direct, communicative, and honest, without being toxic.

Just like with everything else, I think real, authentic communication will be key.

Needing others isn't codependence

Needing others is a human thing. It's who we are, and what we do. We formed society and language to survive together. Not that we have to stick to history, but I think it's easy to see what happens when people are lonely and isolated. People feel a deep trauma from isolation. It can lead to so many other issues, including PTSD, being groomed into membership in fascist and white supremacist terrorist groups like the Nazis/KKK/Proud Boys, being groomed into cults, self-harm, and more.

Yet here we are, pushing this narrative for centuries that you have to pull yourself up by your bootstraps. You know, the saying created to mean "you can't do the impossible"? The saying that is constantly misused and abused? It goes further. People tell you that you can't love others until you fully love yourself. They spout that you shouldn't need others or else you're codependent. These are all the same ideas.

I can tell you right now, we all deserve love, and need community. Even before we are perfect and love ourselves perfectly. As much as I've talked about learning to love myself, it was while I also had a community around me. I was working with mental health professionals. I was loved by friends and family. I had a support network.

That doesn't mean I wasn't lonely. I had issues that I needed to sort out in myself that were due to self-hatred. I needed to work on these issues for my own self-love and self-worth. Even so, I never once deserved loneliness. I did not have to earn love from others, and ideas centered on earning love, are cruel.

No one owes us anything ever.* That's why you cannot put all of your eggs in one basket, right? You still deserve love, though, you just need to ensure that you have a network. You need community, not just yourself. You need community, not just you and a single other person that you put all of this weight onto.

This shouldn't be new to anyone. These are things that make sense, that marginalized communities, especially Black and Indigenous communities, talk about a lot. And these are things we all feel deeply about.

We just have a lot of bad programming from a white-centered hyper-individualistic society. This bad programming keeps us isolated, to maintain control. If we're lacking in love, and support, we're easily manipulated.

We need a wealth of different relationships to feel secure. We need friends and family. We need greater communities to be a part of, though, stay away from cults and white supremacy, please. As for some of us, we need romantic relationships too. Some people do not, or find fulfillment in other intimate and close relationships that aren't necessarily romantic. Shout out to my aromantic friends!

We need a balance. Self-reflection and our own space to do our own things, while also having different relationships. We should not isolate, as that can cause serious harm to the person in isolation**, and we cannot place expectations on others, right? That's why we need to be around people who want to be in our lives and have a lot of fulfilling relationships in many ways, whatever ways sound good to us.

We learn what our boundaries and needs our through reflection, *while* still deserving love and friendship and community. You are not codependent for wanting love, friendship, passion, and community. You are human.

"Ok, but you've said that you shouldn't make someone into your savior. You've said that it was unfair that you placed all of that expectation on them."

Yes. We need people, we need positive, compassionate, supportive people in our lives. At the same time, it needs to be a community. It needs to be a network of mutual support. You do not need to place all of that on one person, and one kind of relationship.

You may even think that you are not doing that, "I have friends, so that doesn't apply to me!" Meanwhile, you think poorly of yourself and crave the validation of someone else. You hope they will provide for all of your security and happiness. You sit surrounded by those friends, constantly checking the phone for that one person to see if they've reached out. Of course, that can happen when you have a crush or like someone platonically and it's all new. You're excited, after all! The issue is when it's your only source of happiness or validation or positive mood.

You need people, in a balanced way. At least, this is where I'm at right now. I am not an expert. I am not perfect. I might be mistaken, and that's ok. It's all a learning process.

Right now, I am seeking balance, that Temperance. I want my own sense of security and validation, while also being surrounded by supportive, loving people. I am recognizing the feelings that I have, while ensuring that they do not control me. I still honor them, though. I work with them to communicate. I work with them to learn and set boundaries. I work with them to advocate for my needs. Through them, I also see how lovable I am. I also learn to reflect that internal understanding outward with the people in my life.

It is a form of alchemy. It is a form of balance and seeking peace. A way to love myself and others, while allowing others to love me, all in a way that is centered and secure, through what is an anarchistic lens. A way that is harder than it sounds. A way that will be a road full of pitstops, detours, and potholes. A way where I learn and grow, with others, in mutual accountability, communication, trust, and respect. Oh, and of course, love.

You deserve this too, and I hope you find love like this.

* *"No one owes us anything" is a phrase meant to help us break free from abusive cycles, where people use expectations and social norms and empathy to their advantage to harm others. However, this doesn't mean you just stop being empathetic either. If you get red flags, you don't owe them anything. If this is a relationship you care about, then that relationship will take some collaborative effort to work, or it will fall apart. If that relationship is abusive, manipulative, and/or controlling, please leave, in a way that is safe for you to do so. Your safety is paramount. I say this not for people*

being harmed, but because now I'm seeing manipulative people use "No one owes you anything" to explain why their lack of empathy is ok, and that's not what that was for.
** I had this written a bit differently, and what I had didn't really fit. I want to add some context, still, that this is something we have seen again and again—the loss of community, of support, of acceptance, can lead to some really harmful and traumatic experiences, and in some cases, death. I experienced this in my own life, where there were many times that isolation, feeling disconnected from those around me and even myself, and being so utterly and completely alone at certain times in my life led to suicidal ideation.

Please, check in on your loved ones if they are in isolation, and show love and support to those who lose community for just being their authentic selves. Autistic, ADHD, and Transgender people are at a higher risk of suicide than many other people, not due to regret like hateful people would tell you, but because of a lack of support and community.

Needs aren't needy

When you've spent large chunks of your life being gaslit, manipulated, and putting in the emotional labor for others, you begin to think your needs make you "needy". It's one of the first things manipulative or emotionally immature people say, "stop being so needy!!" They can not handle them. They're not in a place to understand your needs, let alone their own. In the end, they get defensive and lash out.

So you bury your emotions and needs. You people please. You do what makes others happy and don't listen to what you want, or what you need.

You are not needy, and you deserve to have people in your life that meet your needs.

Of course, there is nuance. There always will be, as much as I would love the world to be matter of fact. I would love to have perfect social rules that are easy to understand and everyone follows. I would love direct and honest communication every time.

Unfortunately, that's not how it works. And if you're like me and you've had too many people manipulate you, even direct communication can feel off! Some people will not be able to or want to meet your needs. Some won't care about your needs. And sometimes we can be selfish in our needs when we blur the idea that our needs should remove autonomy or boundaries. "Call me every X number of minutes you're out with your friends" is not a need, that's controlling behavior. "Message me when you get home safely" is a need.

This is where it's important to understand our actual needs, through self-reflection. If I think, "I feel insecure when *they* do XYZ", and I don't reflect on that and figure out some base need, I might become controlling. And I have been. And I've been controlled too. So now, when I have my wits about me, I spend time investigating that feeling. I learn what I need, and effectively communicate it.

Let's say that you feel insecure about one of your friends. "They spend so much more time with them than me!" I am using a bit of my own pain from an ex long ago to help illustrate a point.

What's really going on here? First, we're comparing ourselves to others, that's always going to cause insecurity. Second, we clearly want to spend more time with them. Why not ask to have more time, like "Hey, can we go on a date tomorrow?" Boom, you get to spend more time with them. Third, is it really about the friend, or are you afraid you're not important to them? You can ask about that too. "Sometimes, I feel a bit insecure about myself and us. I've had issues in the past, and I would like more affirmations from you on how you feel about me. Are you ok with letting me know how you feel about me a bit more often, and what you appreciate about me?"

I don't know about you, but that sounds a lot better than "I want you to spend less time with them and more time with me!" You express your feelings and needs. At the same time, you still respect that they are their own independent, autonomous person, with their own lives.

You ask them to meet you where you need, rather than commanding or controlling or trying to mess with their life.

This is not just for romantic relationships, you can do this in any relationship. You can communicate needs with friends, family, coworkers, with anyone, really. It won't be easy at first, and you'll make mistakes. Especially if you've had people you trusted deny, ignore, or ridicule your needs in the past. I make mistakes and still do.

You owe it to yourself and those in your life to find ways to healthily communicate your needs. And you know what? If people don't like it, maybe that means that you need to sort out what the relationship is. Maybe then you can negotiate things in a way that works for both of you, or maybe you can't. Maybe it doesn't work out, and that sucks, and now you have to heal that pain. And that's ok too.

Lastly, remember that this comes out of love for them, and for yourself. This comes from a desire to create a stronger connection that works for both of you. This should be a way to expand that love for each other, not control someone.

Fuck fragility

People get so mad at being told that what they did was hateful and bigoted. They can't handle the words "racist", "misogynistic", "homophobic", "transphobic", or " ableist". They decide that they could never be *that*, that is for someone *really* hateful, that's not *them*. It doesn't matter if someone says, "this hurts me, this is harmful". They have made up their mind. They become defensive because they can't bother to understand how their behaviors harm others.

We need to stop thinking "I did something bad therefore I'm a bad person." We also need to stop thinking, "This isn't hateful, this is a difference of opinion, because I don't think it is." Instead, we need to think "Oh, I didn't realize this was harmful, I am sorry! I made a mistake, and I need to learn. I need to make amends. I will unlearn old ways of thinking, and learn to be kinder and more empathetic." If we change how we treat others and remove our identity from "I am good and know best" to "I take accountability and am improving and learning", our interpersonal relationships would be a lot easier and less manipulative.

It's that same fragility from any kind of abuser, right? ***DARVO. Deny, Attack, Reverse Victim and Oppressor.*** It comes from a place of "I cannot be wrong." It comes that needs to remain safe and comfortable, and anything that feels like a threat to that is bad. It says, "I feel unsafe from what I perceive as an attack, like being told I've hurt someone, so I need to initiate a trauma response." We need to become resilient, instead of taking these as attacks, when they're not.

It was when I sat in that uncomfortable place, that I started healing. I let myself be wrong. I acknowledged that I hurt others with my bigotry and indoctrinated ignorance. I let go of my fragility. I was finally open to healing myself, and how I relate to others. This is how we heal and form healthy communities. This is how we work towards fighting systems of oppression like white supremacy and fascism.

I still have a ways to go. My current problem is that I often try to position myself as "not racist". "I'm not like those other white people..." I know, it's fucking embarrassing. It is not anti-racist, just pontificating and identifying as "a good person." I still have biases to challenge. I still have privileges in ways others do not. I still have work to do, and probably will for the rest of my life.

This work is necessary, though, if we're ever going to end oppression. We need to challenge our biases and bigotry. We need to start healing and treating each other better.

Friendship

To walk hand in hand
With a friend you love
Bliss
To feel…accepted
Appreciated
Seen
Hours become minutes
Before you know it
You have to leave
Sadness
What a beautiful day
Gratitude
But I'm selfish
I want this day to last longer
The healing power of understanding
Of respected boundaries
Proper communication
I appreciate you deeply
And I am so happy we met

Why do you want love?

Why do you want love, do you think it will rescue you?

No. I still have my own healing to do.

Why do you want it then?

Why not?

Answer the question.

To not be so alone in a lonely universe. To feel connection and feel like that love actually exists and isn't just something made up. To share my excitement and drama and terror and happiness and desire and snacks.

Snacks?

Yeah, duh. Sharing snacks is better than snacking alone, it's science.

So you want love to share...snacks.

That's reductive, but partially. Travel and see the world, wake up in a cottage by a lake with the person or people you love most, drinking coffee you hate because it's bitter on the dock looking at the water. But it's so serene because you're with someone or maybe multiple someones you want to share all of your experiences with. When did it become so bad to want all of that, to want love, to want closeness? When did this become codependency and we all have to be so fucking hyper-independent and self-made people pulling ourselves up by our bootstraps and not sharing tools and skills and resources and lives and laughter and food.

You think about food a lot.

It's one of the best parts of existence.

Fair point. So you want community?

Yes. That's love too.

And some idea of romance and partnership?

Yes. And I think that's ok, I feel I've been gaslighting myself into thinking that's codependent because of how little closeness I've felt, but it's just fucking human, right? It's like I heard some psychoanalytic buzzword along the way and decided that that must be me. At the same time, I am still healing. I'm still building my own sense of self-love and security and happiness. I just don't want to do that under isolation anymore.

Community

We have this giant societal emphasis on healing alone. Cope alone. Do everything alone. Even the hotlines tell you to go journal and have a bath. Alone.

Here's the thing, we absolutely need personal coping skills, but we also need support systems. We need community. And I feel that people are isolating themselves more and more because of capitalism, and I am concerned about what will happen to us. We started building social networks and communities online. We were finding ways to connect across the world! Then what? These platforms stop pushing your content in favor of more capitalist ads. You're now technologically isolated because they don't like you or what you have to say. You're isolated because you're not important to them—selling is.

Certain platforms are better about this, things like Discord, Mastadon, and MightyNetworks help build communities without an algorithm interfering. These are becoming a digital community center, a notice board, and a way to share ideas and support. This is crucial, when so many physical community places like parks, community centers, town halls, cafes, etc., are closed. Small businesses, like barber shops and salons, where whole civil rights movements were shaped and planned are closed down. Why? Because no one can pay the exorbitant rent to an already exceptionally wealthy conglomerate. The place of community in our lives is important for surviving the threat of a system built to put the wealthy over the rest of us.

The problem? Public owned and run community spaces cost money*. The other problem? There is strength in numbers.

This is by design, the less that people can organize and commune together, the less they can fight against oppression from higher in the socioeconomic hierarchy. The less they commune, the more isolated. The more isolated, the easier to manipulate into buying. The more isolated, the easier to force people to buy things they could share with each other, instead of owning one per household. The more isolated, the higher the chance that you need a job that can extort you because where can you go? Who will help you?

This is how a cult works. Isolate you from support structures. Force you to buy into the cult wholesale. Extort you for value, while pretending that they are giving you what you need.

If you fail? You're the problem. You can't do it on your own. Pay for support. Pay for tools to help. Pay for professionals to take care of you. Pay pay pay pay pay.

The alternative? Building a strong community where people help one another. You still have bills and work, and that isn't going away. Luckily, though, now you have people you can trust. You have people you can lean on in a crisis. You have people who can help you stay successful in a society that demands too much of you.

Easy peasy, right? No. This will require less individualistic models of thought. You cannot apply the hyper-individual ideals of Capitalism and certain spiritual movements that push isolation and restriction over boundaries and interdependence. Yes, you still need boundaries, and some people you might need to cut out of your life, but everyone? Some of these movements act as though any small infraction demands you cut someone out. "They no longer serve you", as if relationships are transactional. "You don't need people like that, you're a Divine Feminine in search of a Divine Masculine" as if the nuclear family is what we need. "It's regardless of sex and gender." Ok, yeah, relationships are great, but you need a community, not just two of you in a home and maybe a family. That's still the nuclear family. More isolation again.

Some talk about "soul family." I like that, though, then they will tell you to remove all people you have in your life right now. Sounds rather cultish again, right? I'm all for removing assholes, I have had to too, but guess what? That can be exceptionally lonely if you were relying on them for things. I'm not saying stay in a bad situation, I'm saying cut people out safely. I'm saying maybe you don't need to cut people out, that should be the last thing you try after all else fails. That is, again, it's a matter of safety. Too many people talk about community and soul family and do not have the social skills to handle conflict. You will be hurt by people. Things will go wrong. You will have to deal with that, and cutting someone out cannot be the only tool you have for conflict resolution.

We made cutting people out our end all be all because of that same hyper-individualism from capitalism. It's a necessary tool, but don't start looking at everything as a nail because you have a hammer. For cases where it isn't abuse, including bigotry which is abusive and violent, then you need to rely on other tools. Wonderful tools like setting boundaries, listening, speaking honestly and without assumption and judgment, and other forms of communication are good for conflict without violence like manipulation or coercion.

You need to learn reformative models of justice, over retributive forms. Otherwise, you will keep being isolated in a world where isolation is more and more synonymous with the inability to survive.

Community spaces don't always cost money, there are ways to use community volunteering and effort to get it working. The problem is, in a hyper-individualistic, and capitalistic, system, we tend to move away from that, as we are busy or don't want to. This means we need money to build and operate these spaces, which means things that are not profitable are deprioritized, over things that are. Plus some people really seem to hate taxes, even though they love the parks that are made with them.

Last Words

Caelynn Margaret Harper

All good things must come to an end.

Understanding...and a fear of obligation

Some part of me is terrified that after people read this book, they will reach out to me. They will feel guilty, sad, hurt, or empathetic, and want me to know they care. The thing is, I do know, it's just that a life of loneliness and trauma comes with pain. I don't want people to reach out due to some kind of negative feeling or obligation. I want them to reach out because they enjoy my company. And I know they do, and will, at the right time. They often do. I am invited to events, and I am asked to dinner. Even so, sometimes, I'm lonely.

This isn't something easy to fix, and it isn't fixed only by having company. Especially company that only want to spend time because they feel they have to. Although I do appreciate the care and the thought behind it. It just feels inauthentic and forced, and that doesn't help anyone feel more connected.

I don't hate anyone who hurt me. I don't hate anyone for neglect or abandonment. I really don't. I may be angry sometimes and keep my distance to protect myself. Every now and again, I need that time alone to recharge and heal. At the same time, I know for most people, it was never done out of malice. They were just as hurt as I was. They have their own healing to do, and I hope they do.

The thing is, being hurt doesn't mean you're allowed to hurt others. At some point, you have to see how you affect others and heal. I'm also not obligated to spend time with people who hurt me, regardless of who they are. At the same time, I totally understand other people who are healing that *do* hate those who hurt them. That anger is completely understandable. We all process things in our own ways, in our own time. I have felt that rage too.

That's why I wrote this book, not to guilt people into spending time with me, or feeling bad about how things went–I want to heal. And I cannot heal by lying about what happened or how I feel. I cannot heal by holding it all in. I have to get it out, and while I could have left it all in my own journals, I didn't. I didn't because I'm hoping people read this, and want to heal for themselves. I want them to heal whether they know me, or they're a stranger from halfway across the world. I want us to all start healing, and that begins with vulnerability, honesty, and feeling the difficult feelings. That begins by owning our fullest experience.

I'm not a doctor, I'm not a therapist, and as such, I cannot tell you how best to heal. I cannot tell you who to love. I can't decide which situations are helping or hurting you. I cannot give you some secret formula or some intricate panacea that will make you feel better. I wish I could. I wish I could for myself too.

What I can do, is show you what I have done. I can show you how I have been processing my pain, my emotions, my own past actions and how I've been harmful. I can show you how I've learned to understand my own needs and boundaries. I can show you a process I have done, and will do, until my last breath. Maybe that will help you do the same. Maybe it will not. Every journey is different. Regardless, you deserve to heal. I think we all have carried enough.

Isn't it time we were vulnerable, honest, open, communicative, and worked towards building community? This rigid individualism where we cut ties with every inconvenience, where we hold it all in, where we blame everyone else for everything, where we keep hurting each other and abusing each other and lashing out, isn't it time for that to end?

Yes, sometimes, you will have to walk away. Sometimes, you will have to call people out. However, there is a difference between accountability and communication, versus gaslighting someone into believing they are the cause of your issues.

I can call out capitalism, the patriarchy, Christianity, white supremacy, colonialism, and those that hurt me and others. That is not blame, that is honest accountability. The blame that we should avoid is when we know someone isn't at fault but we want someone to point to as the cause of the issue anyways. Maybe we drink too much and are a jerk, so we lash out and say it was everyone else's fault at that party. It wasn't.

In the end, we need honesty. We need communication, We need vulnerability, to move forward in a way that builds us all up, instead of tearing others down. And sometimes that requires holding people accountable, including ourselves.

This is why I wrote this. Not to blame, not to shame, not to get more people to reach out, but to show a way out of pain and trauma. I hope I have built an understanding.

One more thing, it will be messy, I mean, look at this

book! You are probably sitting there like "I mean, it sounds like you blame some people in some of these works, Caelynn." You would be right. At the time that I wrote some of these journal entries, poems, and reflections, I absolutely did.

That's the thing about healing, you start from a place of anger, hatred, pain, sorrow, and you feel that, and you process that. Then you look at it, thinking, "shit, I've done some of this too." You then process that pain, sorrow, and anger at yourself. You understand you didn't do that because of malice, but because of suffering. It doesn't make it ok, it just is. This isn't to find an excuse, but an explanation that provides you with a treatment plan, right? Explanations are not excuses, as some claim. They're the why that helps us understand how to move forward.

After you've done this reflection, you look at the actions of others toward you. Guess what? You see that same pattern, that they did it due to suffering too. Due to this, for me, in some cases I forgave, and let go. Other times, I still hold that pain. That's not to say you have to forgive, you **absolutely** do not have to, there are many ways to grieve, process, and release. This is just one way that I did, as it worked for me. Or maybe it's people pleasing still. Or I'm tired and I just want to drop it in my mind. Who knows.

You might not be able to forgive, and that is ok. You don't have to in order to heal, to learn, to grow. Find whatever works for you in order to heal, and know that it will be messy at times, like mine was. That's another reason I wrote this. I want you all to see how messy and difficult healing can be, but to know that it will be worth it. It will help you build community and draw in amazing things into your life. It will help you keep out the things that are not good for you.

I hope you heal.

A gentle reminder

I am loved, even though some people in my past did not love me.

I am worthy of love, even though some people treated me like I was not.

I am surrounded by love now, even though I was not always.

I have wonderful people in my life, as they are; I do not need them to be any different, unless I need an unkind behavior to change.

I welcome every kindness, every loving gesture, every gift, as expressions of love, and I do not need to wonder about them further.

I take people as they say they are, without suspicion. If something seems off, I can note it, and see if they reveal more about themselves. I don't need to guess at the future, I can see them as they present now.

I will communicate how I feel, what I want, what I need, and set healthy boundaries. I will listen, and respect others' needs, wants, feelings, and boundaries. I will walk away from people who disrespect mine.

I do this, to be authentic in every relationship, platonic

or otherwise, without expectation, without worry, without control.

I do this to show love, and accept love, in all areas of my life, each and every day.

The end...or the middle?

This is the end. Or, rather the middle. I am not dying, after all. Healing is ongoing. It takes time and effort. That sounds exhausting, right? It is, if you do not carve out time for joy, celebration, wonderment, curiosity, inspiration, creation, and pleasure. You need some respite from the grief, pain, frustration, sorrow, and trauma.

I am an ever-changing work of art. I see that now. I am the art, and the artist. The dream and the dreamer. The creation and the creator. I believe we are all art and the artist. I am not the first to think of myself as a work of art, nor will I be the last. I just finally see it. All of this work, the erasing and the redrawing, the smushing of an improperly thrown clay pot on the wheel to throw it again, melting down a poorly cast metal sculpture to recast it—that is me.

I am wonderfully grateful and crying with joy that I have seen that my work was not in vain. The bigotry, anger, and sexism I let go from the church and some of the adults in my life. The self-loathing, projection, and jealousy that was vitriol is now an impetus for healing. Seeing myself, my childhood, and my life throughout, as it really was, or as close as I can even through my point of view. Knowing who I truly am. Becoming my real self by shedding all of that miasma.

Seeing people I barely know smile at me because they see the joy I have most days. Happy conversations with people I've never met who help me see how wonderful I am. Understanding how far I have healed. I know that there will still be painful moments. There will be bigots. There will be hatred and misgendering. There may even be physical violence instead of just verbal violence. Through it all, I know, *I know,* I am walking down the right road out of the crossroads.

I hope that you can find your way through the crossroads too.

With love,
Caelynn Margaret Harper

Caelynn Margaret Harper

Last Notes

Last Notes

Sources

Madrigal-Borloz V., Practices of so-called "conversion therapy": Report of the Independent Expert on protection against violence and discrimination based on sexual orientation and gender identity** (A/HRC/44/53*). UN Human Rights Council https://documents-dds-ny.un.org/doc/UNDOC/GEN/G20/108/68/PDF/G2010868.pdf

Inanna. (2023, January 12). In Wikipedia. https://en.wikipedia.org/w/index.php?title=Inanna&oldid=1132467123

Leick, Gwendolyn (2013) [1994], Sex and Eroticism in Mesopotamian Literature, New York City, New York: Routledge, ISBN 978-1-134-92074-7

Roscoe, Will; Murray, Stephen O. (1997), Islamic Homosexualities: Culture, History, and Literature, New York City, New York: New York University Press, ISBN 978-0-8147-7467-0

Andrew R. Flores, Ilan H. Meyer, Lynn Langton, Jody L. Herman, "Gender Identity Disparities in Criminal Victimization: National Crime Victimization Survey, 2017-2018", American Journal of Public Health 111, no. 4 (April 1, 2021): pp. 726-729.

About the author

Caelynn Margaret Harper writes, reads tarot, hoards books, creates and plays games, and loves to cook delicious food. She loves to create as much as she can. She is surrounded by love from incredible people, her aptly named and mischievous cat Loki, and herself as well. She is actively choosing to heal and love herself, and hold herself accountable, in all the ways she deserves.

She spent most of her childhood building fantastic worlds in her imagination, playing video games, and riding her bike to the local grocer to get soda and candy. She went to school at a Christian parochial school, where she was liked by some, and bullied by others for being different. She was "one of the girls", often giving advice in grade school relationships, and life, even back then. She was also punished by authority and peers alike for her difficulties in communicating, knowing when and when not to talk, and what the social norms of many situations were. This continued well into her time at an Evangelical Lutheran high school and college. She also was not perfect, was at times an asshole, and was justifiably treated as such.

She eventually left that school, the church, and began drinking heavily and escaping reality in her 20's. There were a lot of ups and downs, some good relationships that ended because they were untenable and doomed from the start. Other relationships and situationships were terrible, both due to others' behaviors, and her own. She was unpacking all of the ways her conservative Christian upbringing had affected her beliefs, opinions, thoughts, and actions. But still, she spent too much time escaping through drinking.

In therapy, accountability, and through further self-reflection and unpacking bigotry and the patriarchy, she has found love and peace. She has found ways to take care of herself, in order to be the best version of herself, for herself and her loved ones. She realized how much about herself she was ignoring, denying, and hiding. She is not done, as healing is a lifelong journey, one of constant presence and understanding, choosing love whenever you can.

She invites you to do the same. Own up to your mistakes and harm. Understand your emotions and traumas. Heal, protect, and love yourselves, and move forward being kinder.

www.ingramcontent.com/pod-product-compliance
Lightning Source LLC
Chambersburg PA
CBHW030816190426
43197CB00036B/496